BANKRUPTING JOE THE TAXPAYER

WITH NO ONE TO BAIL HIM OUT

BY D.J. GOLIO

authorHOUSE®

AuthorHouse™
1663 Liberty Drive
Bloomington, IN 47403
www.authorhouse.com
Phone: 1-800-839-8640

First published by AuthorHouse 8/14/2009

ISBN: 978-1-4389-7856-7 (e)
ISBN: 978-1-4389-7854-3 (sc)
ISBN: 978-1-4389-7855-0 (hc)

Printed in the United States of America
Bloomington, Indiana

This book is printed on acid-free paper.

TABLE OF CONTENTS

CHAPTER 1

TAX WAKE-UP CALL

The idea of writing a book that reveals the tremendous invisible tax burden on Americans started several years ago. I opened up a monthly Verizon telephone bill covering charges for a second land line into my home in case of a power failure, since my principal telephone service provider was Cablevision. To my complete surprise, the bill for the month was $38.52. This was the charge for a very basic service line that had little local usage, one local call every two days, less than one call per day covering my region, and nine itemized long-distance calls.

I studied this bill very carefully, trying to understand how the charge for the month got up to $38.52; to my surprise, it was all the taxes spread out in every category of the bill driving the cost up. A photocopy of this bill follows after the narrative explanation, but the details and similar charges on the Verizon bill will be found in telephone bills throughout the country.

Under the category "Verizon Basic Local Services," I found:

1- Monthly charge for the Dial Tone was $11.85

2- Verizon Local Calls amounted to $1.35

3- Surcharges and Taxes amounted to $11.28

The total for this group was $24.48, with 46 percent of the total representing government-mandated or direct tax charges consisting of a Federal Communications Commission "FCC" Line Access Charge, Federal USF Surcharge, another Surcharge on the Charge and Surcharge, 911 Surcharge, Federal Tax and NY State/Local Sales Taxes.

The FCC Line Access Charge billed by our local telephone companies is actually the result of a federal government-mandated program to subsidize telephone service in sparsely populated areas. I would bet that most readers did not know a thing about this item at all.

At this point, I am wondering how it came to be that all these taxes managed to find their way into my very simple monthly telephone bill. More importantly, where was the old Public Service Commission to protect the consuming public from runaway pricing for very necessary and vital services such as the telephone, electricity, natural gas, and the like.

Looking down on the bill to the next category, "Verizon Calls," there was:

    4- Regional Calls $4.76

    5- Pay-Per-Use Services $0.75

    6- Surcharges and Taxes $0.91

The next grouping, entitled "Verizon Optional Services," was blank with the final group shown as "All Other Charges":

    7- 8-Verizon Long Distance $7.62

All of the above line-item amounts make up the month's total of $38.52, inclusive of all taxes and surcharges collected for the various federal, state, and local government agencies. See Verizon exhibit below:

Bankrupting Joe The Taxpayer

How to Reach Us: See page 2

Account Summary

Previous Charges	$75.51
Payment Received Aug 24. Thank You.	-75.51
Past Due Charges	$.00
New Charges	
(page 3)	$30.90
Long Distance (page 4)	7.62
Total New Charges Due October 2	**$38.52**
Total Due (Past Due + New)	**$38.52**

These monthly charges are for your service from
September 07 to October 06.

1-866-VZ-MOVES

Moving? 1-866-VZ-MOVES

*Across the street or across the
nation, one call can do it all.
Call us for Internet, phone and
entertainment in your
new home.*

Help Keep Internet Access Tax-Free

*If Congress doesn't act by
November 1, the government can start
taxing your Internet access.
Log on to
donttaxourweb.org/actnow/
to learn more and to help keep
the Internet tax-free.*

**Complete A Survey For A Chance
To Win A MOTORAZR Maxx Ve Phone**

*Complete a survey & you'll be entered
for a chance to win a Motorola
MOTORAZR maxx Ve phone.
Go to Verizon.com/billsurvey
for rules & to complete your survey.
Surveys must be completed by 10/15/07.
One survey per household.*

▼ Detach & return payment slip with your check, payable to Verizon.

New Charges Due: 10/02/07

Total Due $38.52   090707

Amount Paid:

$ ☐☐.☐☐

PO BOX 1100
ALBANY NY 12250-0001

New Charges

⁕Detail provided in the Itemized Calls section of the bill.

Basic Local Services

1	Monthly Charge for Dial Tone		$11.85
2	Verizon Local Calls*		1.35
3	Surcharges and Taxes		11.28

FCC Line Charge	$6.39	911 Surcharge	$ .35
Federal USF Surcharge	$ .72	Federal Tax	$ .61
Surcharge(s)	$ .81	NY State/Local Sales Tax	$2.40

Total   **$24.48**

Calls

4	Regional Calls*	$4.76
5	Pay-Per-Use Services*	.75
6	Surcharges and Taxes	.91

Federal Tax	$.03	Surcharge(s)	$.23
NY State/Local Sales Tax	$.65		

Total   **$6.42**

Optional Services

7	All Call Blocking	$.00

Total   **$.00**

All Other Charges

8	Long Distance	see detail pages	$7.62

Total   **$7.62**

ITEMIZED CALLS

Local Calls

Refer to your phone book for rates and discount information.

With message rate service you pay a set price for each local call you make no matter how long you talk.

no.	place called	charge per call	number of calls	period	amount
9	L.Westch	9.0¢	10	day	
10			1	eve	
11			4	ngt	
Total					$1.35

Regional Calls

Your average price per minute is 17.0¢.

no.	place called	rate period	number of calls	rate per minute	number of minutes	amount
11	U.Westch	day	1	17¢	3	$.51
12	Nassau	day	1	17¢	5	.85
13	W.Suffolk	day	2	17¢	20	3.40
Sub-Total					28	$4.76
Total						$4.76

Pay-Per-Use Services

Detail

no.	date	time	feature
14	8/16	2:02pm	Busy Redial

Line Summary

no.	feature	total number of activations	number of activations billed	charge per activation	Pay-Per-Use charge
15	Busy Redial	1	1	$.75	$.75
Total for Line					$.75

Total Pay-Per-Use Services   **$.75**

Long Distance

Long Distance Summary

1. Plans and Other Charges		0.48
2. Itemized Calls		6.80
3. Surcharges and Taxes		0.34
Total		**$7.62**

Long Distance Plans and Other Charges

4. Basic Rates		0.00
5. Federal Universal Service		0.48
Total		**$0.48**

Long Distance Surcharges and Taxes

6. NY State/Local Sales Tax		0.12
7. NY Gross Receipts Tax Surcharge		0.18
8. NY Metropolitan Transit Auth. Surcharge		0.04
Total		**$0.34**

Long Distance Itemized Calls

no.	date	time	place	number	rate period	min.	amount
9.	8/20	10:52am			Peak	2.0	0.80
10.	8/20	11:01am			Peak	1.0	0.40
11.	8/20	11:03am			Peak	1.0	0.40
12.	8/20	6:10pm			Offpeak	1.0	0.40
13.	8/21	3:55pm			Peak	4.0	1.60
14.	8/30	9:23pm			Offpeak	5.0	2.00
15.	9/02	1:44pm			Offpeak	1.0	0.40
16.	9/05	5:03pm			Peak	1.0	0.40
17.	9/06	5:20pm			Peak	1.0	0.40
						17.0	6.80
						17.0	6.80
Total of all Itemized Calls						**17.0**	**6.80**

By the way, the telephone excise tax is one on the nation's oldest taxes originally imposed on the wealthy as a "war tax" or "luxury tax" to help finance the Spanish-American War. Naturally, at that time, there were no income tax revenues to fund the war, and only the wealthy could afford telephones. This tax continued to fund just about every war since 1898, when it was first enacted, through the Vietnam conflict, although for brief periods since its enactment, it was suspended or partially repealed.

Now that I was through the entire Verizon bill detail, I needed to know what percentage of the total bill represented pure Verizon services. The answer was 67.5 percent, with the balance of 32.5 percent representing all the tax-related items embedded in the billing categories. In fact, if I deduct my long-distance charges and related taxes from the totals, the actual tax percentage for the basic services jumps up from 32.5 percent to 37.9 percent.

At this point, I am shocked and feeling quite abused about my discovery. I wonder how extensive this stealth tax assault may be in terms of other essential services, including electricity bills, gas and oil heating bills, water bills, and the like. My curiosity level peaked, I now move on and continue the investigation of the stealth taxes assault by reviewing the Consolidated Edison billing, to see if similar tax or related items were present.

However, before moving on with the investigative results, I would like to point out that the "stealth tax" is generally believed to be a single tax at the federal level named the "alternative minimum tax" or "AMT." This tax was originally conceived of in 1969 by congressional Democrats who attempted to collect taxes from fewer than one hundred millionaires who legally escaped or minimized their tax bills. The number of taxpayers who will be subject to the federal AMT in 2008 is expected to exceed 20 million. I will devote some more time to this subject of AMT later on.

As we all know, our utility bills that come in the mail every month can run from two to a dozen pages or more, listing data that one can only hope to understand.

In the case of the local New York City utility, Consolidated Edison ("ConEd"), I have seen this monthly bill change dramatically over the years. When I was much younger, natural gas was billed in volumes of "one thousand cubic feet" or "mcf." This mcf billing practice continued for many years, while the price of natural gas averaged two dollars per mcf for more than twenty-five years. The price of natural gas was deregulated in 1978, and the prices started to move north of two dollars; the cost of gas transportation also started to increase. Utilities wanted in some way to disguise the increases by using undecipherable terms and formulas that make it difficult to translate usage back to the standard measurement of the mcf. Thus, billing changed to "one hundred cubic feet" or "ccf"; after a while, billing was in "therms," derived using a conversion factor that converts ccf into therms.

Here is what we now see on our ConEd bill each month:

Gas Consumption:

Gas charges are for the gas you used over a thirty-day period plus the cost of getting that gas delivered to you. Gas meters measure the volume of natural gas used in ccf. Gas is billed in therms, which represent the heat content of the gas. What does all this mean? Well, there are different qualities of natural gas; some natural gas is richer, since it has a higher British thermal unit ("Btu") content and therefore is more expensive. The higher the Btu content, the more energy efficiency is realized. This cost must therefore be passed on to you, but how do we know if the Btu content we are billed for is accurate? Averages are no doubt used, so we likely will never really know what the margin of error is in our monthly billing. If they are going to use averages, why not stick with the mcf billing? At least we can then determine what the additional costs are from the wellhead to our homes. I guess that would be too simplistic and perhaps embarrassing, and I will illustrate why, using my most recent ConEd billing.

I was supplied with 73 therms of natural gas at a cost of 145.5890¢ per therm, plus charges for procuring and storing natural gas, credit and collection activities, and cost for customers who do not pay (uncollectible), cost for basic system infrastructure, and all customer-related services, plus adjustment for the variation of normal weather. Translation: the cost per mcf to me was $23.62 before assorted state taxes that added another $1.92, for a total cost of $25.54 per mcf. So now when we read about the cost of a barrel of oil in the $120.00 range and natural gas (per mcf) currently at $8.65 (both prices as of August 2008), at least we can now see and understand once and for all the cost of getting this commodity into our homes.

Electricity Consumption

Electricity charges are a bit more straightforward, since the meter readings are in kilowatt hours ("kWh") and the billing is also in kilowatt hours billed by ConEd at 14.0641¢ per kWh. To this basic charge of electricity supplied to you there is added the standard charge associated with procuring electricity, credit and collection-related activities, the added expense of uncollectible accounts, and let's not forget the tax on ConEd gross receipts from sales of utility services and "other tax surcharges."

Your electricity charges

These charges are for the electricity you used (supply) and getting that electricity to you (delivery). Rates are based on a 30 day period. When your billing period is more or less than 30 days, we prorate your bill accordingly.

Electricity you used during this 30 day billing period from Jun 30, 2008 to Jul 30, 2008
Rate: EL1 Residential or Religious   Meter#

We measure your electricity by how many kilowatt hours (kWh) you use. One kWh will light a 100 watt bulb for 10 hours.

Jul 30, 08 actual reading	6639
Jun 30, 08 actual reading	-3361
Your electricity use	**3,278 kWh**

► Your supply charges

Supply 3,278 kWh @14.0641 c/kWh $461.02
Charge for the electricity supplied to you by Con Edison.

Merchant function charge $15.03
Charge associated with procuring electricity, credit and collection related activities and uncollectible accounts.

GRT & other tax surcharges $4.81
Taxes on Con Edison gross receipts from sales of utility services and other tax surcharges.

Total supply charges   **$480.86**

Your total electricity supply cost for this bill is 14.7¢ per kWh. You can compare this price with those offered by energy services companies (ESCOs). For a list of ESCOs, visit www.PowerYourWay.com or call 1-800-780-2684.

► Your delivery charges

Basic service charge $12.89
Charge for basic system infrastructure and customer-related services, including customer accounting, meter reading and meter maintenance. A billing and payment processing charge of $0.47, *which may be avoided by switching to an energy services company (ESCO)*, is also included.

Delivery 3,278 kWh @6.9561 c/kWh $228.02
Charge for maintaining the system through which Con Edison delivers electricity to you.

SBC/RPS charges @0.2401 c/kWh $7.87
The System Benefits Charge/Renewable Portfolio Standard charges fund New York State renewable energy, environmental and other related public policy programs.

GRT & other tax surcharges $8.74
See earlier definition.

Total delivery charges   **$257.52**

► Your sales tax

Sales tax @6.0000% $44.30
Tax collected on behalf of New York State and/or your locality. *Buying your energy from an energy services company (ESCO) will lower your sales tax.*

Total sales tax   **$44.30**

►► Total electricity charges $782.68

Your average daily electricity use

a year ago

Water Consumption

Many years ago, I recall that most communities had charges for water supply included in their local taxes. The cost for water consumption historically has been very nominal, but this too has changed in the past several years, as state and local governments continue to explore for new sources of revenue. After reviewing in detail my most recent water bill from United Water, I am convinced that their billing format—and the format of most utility bills for that matter—is designed to ensure that the recipient gets disgusted with all the abbreviated terms that are spelled out somewhere in the fine print that no one really gets to read.

To illustrate a frustration that we have all experienced, my United Water bill contains ten separate line items of charges with an assortment of different codes. Actual water consumption is billed in "CCF" or 100 cubic feet, the equivalent of 748 gallons of water.

The first code other than CCF charges was a "PWA Adjust" or Purchased Water Adjustment related to rate increases charged by New York City to United Water after June 30, 2006.

The next code is for a "DIP" charge, covering the cost for developing a new water-supply source mandated by the New York State Department of Health under the Safe Drinking Water Act.

Moving on, the next code listed and labeled as "DEFER PWA" or Deferred Purchased Water rate increases charged by New York City. It would appear that the increases made reference to were already paid by United Water prior to 2006 and now being passed on to customers. I must assume that there were some retroactive pass through rate increases authorized by the Public Service Commission.

The next charge code is "MAIN REP PR," covering the long-term program for improving underground water mains.

The next-to-last code, entitled "RECONCILE," is either a charge or a credit due to adjustments or reconciliations made based upon actual revenues or property taxes

The final code is simply labeled "TOWN TAX."

The "Important Messages" section of the bill had two wonderful surprise messages. One advised me that the Public Service Commission, effective July 28, 2008, changed the LTMRP Surcharge from 2.80 percent to 3.49 percent, *an increase of more than 24 percent* for that one item alone. A second message advised me that the Public Service Commission once again authorized the water purchases from the New York City supply system to increase from 0.1649 cents to 0.2577 cents, *an increase of more than 56 percent*, effective July 1, 2008.

So what is the important message that we as taxpayers get from the water bill narrative facts recited above? A good portion of our federal tax dollars (hundreds of millions) are being sent to Iraq in order to rebuild their infrastructure. This includes water supplies and related delivery systems, and electrical capacity, to name two of the many public works programs underway in that country. Meanwhile, we here in the United States have to pay for the improvement of our own domestic water mains and delivery systems out of our net pay (after payment of federal, state, and local income taxes, a portion of which is used to pay for similar projects in Iraq).

We are all aware that gas, electricity, telephone service, and water are essential in our lives, but how many of us really know about how and when the dramatic increases in rates, taxes, surcharges, and the like are being approved by our representatives in government and the Public Service Commission? This condition causes most of us to have less money for either spending or saving, as our net paychecks buy less each year, despite any increase in our pay rates that generally follow the annual rate of inflation. This is only true, of course, if you are fortunate enough to work for a company that is sensitive to the rising cost of living each year in the first place.

USAGE HISTORY
Quarterly usage in hundred cubic feet

Billing Date:	08/15/08
Account Number:	
Previous Balance	$287.68
Payments Through 08/15/08 *Thank You*	$288.00CR
Balance Forward	$0.32CR
Current Charges **Due 09/04/2008**	$780.63
TOTAL AMOUNT DUE *Paid 9/5/08*	**$780.31**

Next meter reading date: on or about 11/12/2008

*PAY BY 09/04/2008 TO AVOID A 1 5% LATE PAYMENT CHARGE

SERVICE   SERVICE ADDRESS:

Meter Number	Service From	To	Days of Service	Meter Reading Previous	Present	Usage	Unit of Measure	Reading Type	Rate
	05/20/08	08/14/08	86	2649	2845	196	CCF	ACTUAL	WTG
					EQUIVALENT TO	146,608 GALLONS			

12 CCF @ $3.227	$38.72	— DEFER PWA		$17.89
184 CCF @ $3.067	$564.33	— MAIN REP PR		$21.05
WATER CHARGE SUBTOTAL	$603.05	— RECONCILE		$2.69 CR
PWA ADJUST	$50.51	— TOWN TAX		$6.63
DIP CHARGE	$84.19	**TOTAL CURRENT CHARGES**		**$780.63**

SEE REVERSE SIDE FOR IMPORTANT ACCOUNT INFORMATION

IMPORTANT MESSAGES

As authorized by the Public Service Commission, effective July 27, 2008 the LTMRP Surcharge changed from 2.80% to 3.49%. United Water purchases its water from New York City Water Board. As authorized by the PSC, a NYCWB increase from .1649 cents to .2577 per ccf is effective July 1, 2008.
RESIDENTIAL
As authorized by the Public Service Commission, effective January 1, 2008 the RAP Surcredit is 0.446%.
ATTENTION: United Water is forming a Customer Advisory Panel in your community. Help us to serve you better by becoming a CAP member. For more information call (914) 637-5324.

PLEASE DETACH HERE AND RETURN THE BOTTOM PORTION WITH YOUR PAYMENT IN THE RETURN ENVELOPE PROVIDED

UNDERSTANDING YOUR BILL

CONSUMPTION UNIT OF MEASURE
CCF: 100 cubic feet, equivalent to 748 gallons

DEFER PWA-DEFERRED PURCHASED WATER
Rate increases charged by NY City and paid by UW New Rochelle prior to 2006.

DIP CHARGE-DELAWARE INTERCONNECTION PROJECT
Cost for developing a new water supply source mandated by NY State Department of Health through the Safe Drinking Water Act.

MAIN REP PR-LONG TERM MAIN RENEWAL
Long-term program for improving underground water mains.

PWA ADJUST-PURCHASED WATER ADJUSTMENT
Rate increases charged by NY City to UW New Rochelle after June 30, 2006.

RECONCILE-REVENUE AND PROPERTY TAX RECONCILIATION
Charge or credits due to adjustments or reconciliations made based upon actual revenues or property taxes.

SURO3REV-PRIOR REVENUE RECONCILIATIONS
The PSC authorized collection of a prior period reconciliation based on a level of revenues previously authorized.

CUSTOMER READING
A reading of the water meter provided by the customer to the utility.

ESTIMATED READING
A system generated reading based on previous historical readings, when an actual reading could not be taken.

NO ACCESS CHARGE
A charge resulting from a customer's failure to allow the company to access the meter.

CUSTOMER SERVICE

EMERGENCIES
914 632 6900
Available 24/7 for reporting service disruptions or other water emergencies.

BY TELEPHONE
914 632 6900

BY FAX
914 637 5333

IN PERSON / IN WRITING
United Water New Rochelle Customer Service Center
2525 Palmer Avenue
P.O. Box 469
New Rochelle, NY 10801
Monday through Friday (except holidays)
8:00 a.m. - 4:30 p.m.
Always remember to include your account number on any correspondence to us.

BY E-MAIL
UWNRcustomerservice@unitedwater.com

ONLINE
www.unitedwater.com/uwnr

NEW YORK PUBLIC SERVICE COMMISSION
United Water is regulated by the NY PSC. Customers can contact the PSC's Consumer Services Division at:
90 Church Street - 4th floor
New York, NY 10007-2919
800 342 3377
www.dps.state.ny.us

PAYMENT OPTIONS

BY TELEPHONE
To pay your bill by phone, call us at 888 608 6690. *A convenience fee applies for this service.*

BY DIRECT DEBIT
E-Pay is our free direct payment program that automatically deducts your bill payment from your bank account. Call or e-mail us for an application form, or download the form from our website.

IN PERSON
Pay by cash, check or money order during business hours at our Customer Service Center.

BY MAIL
For your convenience, a return envelope accompanies this statement and should be used to make payments by mail. Please include your bill stub to avoid a delay in processing your payment.
DO NOT SEND CASH.

ONLINE
To pay your bill online please visit www.unitedwater.com and click on the Western Union SpeedPay link. *A convenience fee applies for this service.*

GENERAL INFORMATION

RATE SCHEDULE
A rate schedule is available upon request.

EMPLOYEE IDENTIFICATION
All company employees are uniformed and wear identification badges with the company logo, the employee's picture and name, and the date the card was issued. Please ask to see it, or call us to confirm an employee's name.

THIRD-PARTY NOTICE
To prevent unnecessary termination of water service in situations where the customer is ill, incapacitated or away from home, the customer can designate a third party to be informed of any final disconnection notice.

HELPING HAND PROGRAM
Special protections are provided for termination and reconnection of service in cases

Gasoline Excise Taxes

This tax is currently what I would characterize as a real hot button. Everyone in the United States was choking on gasoline prices at the pump for almost three continuous years through the end of 2008, not to mention other energy costs such as home heating oil and natural gas.

Gasoline excise taxes in general consist of federal, state, and local taxes on each gallon of fuel purchased. Many years ago, all the details of the tax were on display at the top of each gas pump, to show what the cut was for each level of government. Today the tax has reached such embarrassing levels that the signs now simply read: "Price per gallon includes all taxes." When the price of a barrel of oil increases so dramatically—as was the case from 2006 through most of 2008—it is difficult for the average person to figure out how much is truly related to the escalating price of oil or higher taxes being collected by every level of our government.

The revenue stream from this tax to the federal, state, and local governments is astonishing. To illustrate, *the estimated take by the states alone for 2007 exceeded $50 billion.* The federal government's estimated take for 2007 was more than $20 billion. Most, if not all, of the federal excise tax collected is earmarked for the federal highway fund that distributes money back to the states for highway projects, repairs, and so on. These amounts exclude local excise taxes in the larger cities such as New York, plus a general sales tax on top of it all.

How does one translate all of this into one amount for the year? Well, if we assume that the average American drives 15,000 miles per year, averaging 20 miles per gallon of fuel, this works out to 750 gallons of gas purchased. The combined average of all taxes loaded into the price per gallon is roughly 56.4¢, including 18.4¢ of federal excise tax, plus state and local excise taxes averaging 38¢. This total of 56.4¢ per gallon is exclusive of local general sales taxes where applicable. Multiplying the 750 gallons purchased by the 56.4¢ results in an annual gasoline-related tax of $423.00 or more than $35.00 per month cash out of pocket. Keep in mind that in many states such as California, New York, Washington, Connecticut, Wisconsin, Pennsylvania, West Virginia, North Carolina, and Nevada, it is more than the average of 56.4¢

I prepared the table below for all states plus Washington, DC, showing what the state gasoline excise tax was as of January 1, 2007 and the increases that some states put in effect as of January 1, 2008.

STATE	1/1/2008	1/1/2007	$ AMOUNT CHANGE	% CHANGE	STATE	1/1/2008	1/1/2007	$ AMOUNT CHANGE	% CHANGE
CA	$ 0.455	$ 0.180	$ 0.275	153%	AK	$ 0.080	$ 0.080	-	0%
FL	$ 0.332	$ 0.153	$ 0.179	117%	CO	$ 0.220	$ 0.220	-	0%
HI	$ 0.326	$ 0.160	$ 0.166	104%	DE	$ 0.230	$ 0.230	-	0%
IL	$ 0.395	$ 0.201	$ 0.194	97%	ID	$ 0.250	$ 0.250	-	0%
MI	$ 0.360	$ 0.190	$ 0.170	89%	LA	$ 0.200	$ 0.200	-	0%
CT	$ 0.441	$ 0.250	$ 0.191	76%	MD	$ 0.235	$ 0.235	-	0%
IN	$ 0.317	$ 0.180	$ 0.137	76%	MO	$ 0.176	$ 0.176	-	0%
GA	$ 0.260	$ 0.152	0.108	71%	NH	$ 0.196	$ 0.196	-	0%
NY	$ 0.412	$ 0.246	$ 0.166	67%	NJ	$ 0.145	$ 0.145	-	0%
NV	$ 0.325	$ 0.248	$ 0.077	31%	NC	$ 0.302	$ 0.302	-	0%
AL	$ 0.202	$ 0.180	$ 0.022	12%	ND	$ 0.230	$ 0.230	-	0%
VA	$ 0.196	$ 0.175	$ 0.021	12%	OH	$ 0.280	$ 0.280	-	0%
MA	$ 0.235	$ 0.210	$ 0.025	12%	OK	$ 0.170	$ 0.170	-	0%
MN	$ 0.220	$ 0.200	$ 0.020	10%	RI	$ 0.310	$ 0.310	-	0%
SD	$ 0.240	$ 0.220	$ 0.020	9%	TN	$ 0.214	$ 0.214	-	0%
ME	$ 0.291	$ 0.268	$ 0.023	9%	TX	$ 0.200	$ 0.200	-	0%
WA	$ 0.360	$ 0.340	$ 0.020	6%	UT	$ 0.245	$ 0.245	-	0%
AZ	$ 0.190	$ 0.180	$ 0.010	6%	VT	$ 0.200	$ 0.200	-	0%
SC	$ 0.168	$ 0.160	$ 0.008	5%	WV	$ 0.315	$ 0.315	-	0%
KS	$ 0.250	$ 0.240	$ 0.010	4%	WS	$ 0.329	$ 0.329	-	0%
OR	$ 0.250	$ 0.240	$ 0.010	4%	WY	$ 0.140	$ 0.140	-	0%
PA	$ 0.323	$ 0.312	$ 0.011	4%	DC	$ 0.200	$ 0.200	-	0%
IA	$ 0.217	$ 0.210	$ 0.007	3%	NM	$ 0.180	$ 0.188	(0.008)	-4%
MT	$ 0.278	$ 0.270	$ 0.008	3%	KY	$ 0.185	$ 0.197	(0.012)	-6%
MS	$ 0.188	$ 0.184	$ 0.004	2%	NB	$ 0.239	$ 0.280	(0.041)	-15%
AR	$ 0.218	$ 0.215	$ 0.003	1%					

While global oil prices were rising to record levels, choking consumers all over the country and the world for that matter, our state-level politicians (not all states, as indicated in the list above) decided to increase the gasoline tax. One must ask why they would do such a thing. Well, one answer is that they are trying to curtail consumption by increasing the price we pay. My response to this is fine, provided you reduce my property or other tax, so if I am reducing my gas consumption, I am not penalized, especially with my home heating bill and other basic living expenses increasing as a result of higher oil prices. This type of action and thinking by our political geniuses is both warped and corrupted, in that the end game is to collect more revenues to keep up with their unchecked spending year after year.

By the way, at a Senate Judiciary Committee dealing with the run-up in gasoline prices, it was revealed that not less than 15 percent of the cost of gasoline at the pump goes for taxes and only 4 percent represents profits for the oil companies.

What are "Excise Taxes" anyway?

Just about every tax other than property taxes resulting from property ownership is an excise tax. It is imposed on events for the purpose of either raising revenues or curtailing a particular behavior.

For example:

— The cigarette (excise) tax imposed on each pack of cigarettes is intended to curtail or stop people from smoking because it is hazardous to their health. Very true, but can it be our politicians are not interested in collecting more tax revenue at the same time? Hard to believe they are so concerned solely about the state of our health. So buying a pack of cigarettes is an event.

— Some portion of the gasoline (excise) tax is imposed on each gallon as described above to curtail our usage. What about the $70 billion of annual revenue generated for the government to spend? What about the people with two or three jobs that require them to drive to stay alive economically? Buying a gallon of gasoline is an event.

— The tax imposed on alcohol is an excise tax, justified of course to limit our consumption, but it is also a huge tax revenue generator. I wonder how much of this particular tax is earmarked for the treatment of alcohol-related diseases or illnesses. I would venture to guess very little, but hope I am wrong.

— Import or duty taxes are a category of excise taxes on the event of importing goods.

Federal excise tax has been around for more than 200 years, older than income, estate, and gift taxes, financing a variety of programs, primarily wars. But only in the last twenty-five years or so has this source of revenue into the federal treasury exploded. Currently, excise tax is imposed on both individual and corporate taxpayers, providing hundreds of billions of dollars to the federal government alone. Remember, state and local governments also impose excise taxes. Consequently, it is impossible for anyone in any way to escape the impact of this tax, since it covers such a broad range of activities, including essential consumable products and services. The tax is passed on to consumers in the form of higher prices.

The United States Constitution gives the power to collect taxes to the Congress. The current tax system setup began in 1913 with the creation of the income tax. During the same period of time in our history, estate and excise taxes were also imposed. The Depression and two world wars made sure that the new taxes would become a permanent burden for all legitimate United States citizens forevermore. The intent of taxes imposed is to produce revenue to enable the government (federal, state, and local) to meet its primary obligations to provide for the defense and security of the country, pay its debts, and provide for the general welfare of the United States, with a substantial portion of excise taxes placed in trust funds for a specific intended use. The current trust funds include:

— <u>Highway Trust Fund</u> gets its funding from the taxes on fuel. The funds are used to finance highway projects.

— <u>Leaking Underground Storage Tank Trust Fund</u> also gets its funding from taxes on most fuels, and is used to pay for the cost of cleaning up storage tank leaks when the responsible party can't be found or does not have the funds to correct the problem.

— <u>Black Lung Disability Benefits Trust Fund</u> is funded from an excise tax on the sales of coal in the United States and helps qualified miners. Coal operators are obligated to reimburse all disbursements made from the fund to their employees or former employees.

In addition to the above-mentioned excise taxes, additional categories taxed include:

• Heavy trucks and trailers that add to the cost of goods and services we purchase as consumers

• Tires for highway vehicles

• A gas-guzzler tax imposed on certain vehicles with low-mileage fuel efficiency

- Communications services, telephone service, pre-paid phone cards, subscriber line charges, directory listings, WATS services, long-distance toll charges, and other related services.

- Domestic and international air travel

- Wagering

- Occupation taxes covering importers and manufacturers

- Firearms and ammunition

- Certain sporting goods

- Oil and chemicals

- Vaccines

- Coal production sales

CHAPTER 2

SEMANTICS

Most people in the United States are too busy fighting the economic terrorism war each day as our disposable income power is being eroded by higher prices for all goods and services in addition to rising taxes imposed by the federal, state, and local governments. No one has the time to research the meaning of the word "wealthy" as used almost daily by the politicians when they tell us that tax increases under consideration will be leveled at the "wealthy" or the "rich." To help everyone out with brief but very important definitions, I have set forth below some very simple explanations of what we all need to understand about the words we hear used so often by our political leaders.

Most people in the United States are acquainted with the simple class system consisting of the "rich," "middle class"—two categories here, "upper" and "lower"—and "poor" with three categories: "working class," "working poor," and "underclass."

Clearly, there are so many variations to this simple system that are discussed and written about, especially by our political leaders and economic data capture entities, one can easily be misled or confused. In the definitions that follow, I attempt to keep it simple.

JOE THE TAXPAYER—Every U.S. taxpaying legal citizen, male or female, small business owner or investor earning a salary or hourly wage or income, irrespective of the amounts they earn in annual compensation.

RICH—Multi-millionaires with annual incomes over $350,000 (minimum) and a household net worth of $1 million or more. This group represents approximately 1 percent of the total population of households in the United States and includes many politicians, top-level executives, celebrities, and the like.

HOUSEHOLD—Households or household income is the most common measure used by the U.S. government agencies and private institutions in gathering income and other economic data. In 2007, there were approximately 117 million households. Members of a household do not have to be related but rather share a common economic fate. Most of the data I have researched places households into five broad categories of gross income, as reported by the U.S. Census Bureau at *www.census.gov:September 20, 2008*

$0 to $25,000—a group representing approximately 28 percent of all households in 2007.

All in this grouping pay no income taxes or have a zero tax liability. However, they do receive income tax refunds each year in the form of credits such as the earned income and child care credits.

$25,000 to $50,000—a group representing approximately 27 percent of all households in 2007. Again, most households in this group have a zero income tax liability once they file their tax returns and claim a refund for their withholdings made throughout the calendar year.

$50,000 to $75,000—a group representing approximately 18 percent of all households in 2007.

$75,000 to $100,000—a group representing approximately 11 percent of all households in 2007.

Please note that the above categories represent 84 percent of all households in the United States. This simply means that 84 percent of all households have a gross income of less than $100,000 per year and collectively they paid less than 15 percent of all income taxes collected in 2007.

$100,000 or more—a group representing the remaining 16 percent of all households in 2007, further broken down into three sub-categories:

—$100,000 to $149,999: a sub-category representing approximately 10 percent of all households in 2007 or 63 percent of the total for the fifth group.

Note: When you add this first sub-category from the fifth group to the total of the other four groups, you then realize that a total of 94 percent of all households in the United States have a gross income of less than $150,000. Keep in mind that this includes all income earners in the household, and taken all together, they paid less than 20 percent of all taxes collected in 2007. Now, that 20 percent number is an amazing statistic that no politician ever wants to discuss, simply because the remaining sub-categories of the fifth group pay some 80 percent of all taxes. This is why one of the presidential candidates during the 2008 campaign claimed that his proposed tax increases will not affect some 95 percent of the households.

—$150,000 to $199,999: another sub-category of the fifth group, representing approximately 3.3 percent of all households in 2007 or 20 percent of the 16 percent for the fifth group.

These two sub-categories together paid approximately 30 percent of all federal income taxes paid and collected in 2007.

—$200,000 to $249,999: another sub-category of the fifth group, representing approximately 1.2 percent of all households in 2007.

—$250,000 and higher: a group representing approximately 1.5 percent of all households in 2007.

These two sub-categories together paid approximately 50 percent of all federal income taxes collected in 2007.

The Census Bureau also reported that:

- 2007 median annual household income was $50,230. This figure represents gross income before any taxes are deducted and includes households with two income earners, husband and wife, domestic partners, and the like.

- 16 percent of all households, some 23.4 million households in total, had annual gross income of $100,000 or more. This same 16 percent paid almost 80 percent of all federal income taxes paid in 2007.

Conclusion: The remaining 93.6 million households paid the balance of the income tax tab for calendar year 2007, representing less than 20 percent of the total income tax collections.

Using the above statistical data for 2007, more than 50 percent of all households wind up with no income tax liability at all for this particular calendar year after child care and earned income credits granted primarily to the first two groups above that together represent 55 percent of all households.

Again, trying to keep things simple and in lay terms, some quick math will tell a reader that if you are paying taxes now as part of the 20 percent group paying the 80 percent of all income taxes paid, you cannot and will not escape any proposed income tax increase in the future. This fact is not debatable, I assure you.

TAXPAYING RICH—Not rich in terms of assets or an annual income in the millions, but rather any household, including one or more income earners, with a gross income of greater than $100,000 simply by being a member of the elite fifth group described above. This is the most misleading area in terms of what our politicians want us to believe and understand. There are many two-earner households with both husband and wife working, and even if they only make $50,000 each in salary, they would likely qualify for the politician's definition of the taxpaying rich, with the joint annual income of more than $100,000—even though they are clearly part of the middle-class grouping of taxpayers as defined by the U.S. Census Bureau at *www.census.gov:September 20, 2008.*

This would mean that while you are classified as middle class (upper) U.S. Census Bureau at *www.census.gov:September 20, 2008* and promised tax relief by our politicians, please don't wait up for the refund check. Why? Well, when the tax relief details are finalized, you will pay additional taxes for sure as part of the politician's definition of the taxpaying rich group.

SUPER-RICH—The top 1 percent of income-earning households that paid more than 40 percent of all federal income taxes collected in 2007. This group has annual gross income in excess of $250,000 and a net worth of more than $1 million.

MIDDLE CLASS—Households with annual incomes in excess of $35,000, with the lower middle class group topping out at $75,000 and the upper middle class group earning over $75,000 annually in gross income and topping out in the range of $200,000.

WORKING CLASS—Households with annual incomes below $35,000.

LEGISLATIVE BRANCH OF U.S. GOVERNMENT (CONGRESS)—The U.S. Senate and the House of Representatives. This branch passes all laws enacted, including raising and lowering of taxes, and where we can drill for oil and natural gas, to name the most important matters of the day. Many people erroneously believe that tax cuts or tax increases are solely the decision of the president, but this is completely false. The president only makes recommendations and proposals to this branch of government. I need to be sure everyone understands this.

CONGRESSIONAL COMMITTEE OF THE CONGRESS—This is a group of congressional representatives who review details and make recommendations on various matters impacting our society as a whole, including the taxes we pay. The group charged in Congress with tax law change-related recommendations is known as the House Ways and Means Committee.

PORK-BARREL SPENDING—A non-essential expenditure loaded into a proposed bill or budget by a member of either the Senate or House of Representatives. Generally, these pork-barrel items are for pet projects in the legislator's state or district, and are usually tainted with some special-interest type of motive that has very limited benefit to the general taxpaying public as a whole.

LINE-ITEM VETO—This is a power sought by many past presidents of the United States in an attempt to limit the amount of pork-barrel spending by members of Congress, to the detriment of all taxpayers. Needless to say, the Congress has resisted granting this tool to the president, as they wish to continue with the long history of such abusive spending.

DISPOSABLE INCOME—The amount of gross household income that remains after all payroll deductions, including federal income tax withholdings, social security tax, Medicare tax, state income taxes (if any, but there are very few states with no income tax), medical premiums, and any other deductions. Using our 2007 household median income amount of $50,230 a simple illustration of what estimated disposable income would be for this level of income shows:

	Annual	Weekly
Gross Income	$50,230	$965.96
Less:		
Federal Income Taxes (withheld)	3,076	59.15
Social Security Taxes (paid)	3,114	59.88
Medicare Taxes (paid)	1,158	22.27
State Income Taxes (withheld)	1,024	19.69
Medical Premiums (paid)	2,400	46.15
DISPOSABLE INCOME	$39,458	$758.80

This disposable income is not to be confused with taxable income, which in most cases will be lower than the $39,458. In this lower taxable income case, a portion or all of the income taxes withheld in the amount of $3,076, as shown above, will likely be refunded when the income tax return is filed.

The disposable income amounts shown in the illustration above are reflecting amounts that would be available for rent, food, clothing, auto expenses, schooling costs, real estate, and other local taxes unrelated to income, entertainment, vacations, and so on. It is easy to see why most households are struggling with no relief in sight and inescapable proposed tax increases on the way. If federal income taxes remain unchanged, your state or local government will likely move quickly after an election to raise state and local taxes necessary to cover endless increases in state spending that bring about state and local budget gaps (revenue shortfalls). This is especially true at this time due to the slowdown in our economy. The economic slowdown—combined with increased fixed costs that include pension expenses for all state and local municipal employees, such as teachers, police, firemen, hospital workers, and so on—seriously exacerbate the problem.

WEALTHY—The term, as used by our politicians, applies to every taxpayer who fits the profile of being one of the top 25 percent of all tax filers. To qualify, all a single taxpayer needs to earn is $53,000. In fact, looking at the categories described earlier in this chapter, a small portion of the third category and all households under the fourth and fifth groups could be referred to as wealthy from a tax point of view.

To qualify for the top 50 percent of all tax filers, you only need to earn $27,000.

The above qualifications place most taxpayers into the politician's definition of "wealthy." Hard to believe, but a true statistical fact to be sure.

ANCHOR BABY—A term used to describe a child born in the United States to illegal immigrants or other non-citizens. This not only includes illegal immigrants already somewhere in the United States, but also a pregnant woman flying in from a foreign country who gives birth to a child during her stay here in the United States, no matter how brief the stay.

NINJA—A mortgage product available (before the financial crisis arrived and up through the spring of 2007) to prospective home buyers, including mostly otherwise unqualified borrowers, with **NO INCOME, NO JOB, NO ASSETS.** This is the type of program that our House of Representatives Banking Committee encouraged many mortgage banks to provide so that poor people could realize the ultimate American dream of home ownership. When many banks crashed and burned, the House Banking Committee members were the first to point fingers at and publicly peel the skin off the faces of banking executives.

SPENDING REDUCTION—This is probably the most misleading term used by our political representatives, since most of the time it is used to describe a lower growth rate for spending.

To illustrate, if the economic growth or inflation rate is 4 percent per year, the government budgets automatically increase their spending by the 4 percent. If the spending increase is only budgeted at 3 percent, this is what is hailed as a decrease in spending funded by our taxes. We should know that spending at all levels of government almost never go down in absolute dollar terms, due to contractual commitments with the respective labor forces, including teachers, firemen, police, sanitation workers, to name a few at the state and local level of government, and all workers on the federal payroll, including politicians and the military.

TAX CREDIT (Federal)—A reduction of your income taxes payable if you engage in certain specified activities required by the government. Many of the current tax credits go to people who pay little or no federal income taxes at all in the first place and are called tax refunds.

For example: If taxpayer A is a single parent and in order to work, needs to incur child care costs, this taxpayer would be entitled to a "child care credit" and also the "earned income credit." The two credits combined could reduce the taxpayer's income tax bill to zero or below zero, resulting in a refund being paid to someone who paid no taxes at all. What a country! Some politicians refer to such credits as tax cuts, but they are really a form of "welfare assistance."

ALTERNATIVE MINIMUM TAX OR "AMT"—This is a tax that ensures households earning in many instances as little as $75,000 per year will pay a minimum amount of income tax, despite having legitimate itemized deductions that would lower the actual tax to be paid.

To illustrate, if the two-income household mentioned earlier earning $100,000 had deductions for home mortgage interest, state income, and local property taxes, medical expenses, contributions to charities, and miscellaneous deductions for work-related expenses that are not reimbursed by the employer, all totaling $35,000, your normal tax bill after four exemptions would be $6,931.00, or an effective rate of 6.9 percent on the gross income of $100,000. The AMT rules will kick in and say that many of your itemized deductions cannot be taken or will be limited in amount because you earned too much money, and therefore AMT tax rate of 28 percent must be used. So if you assume that only $25,000 of your $35,000 in itemized deductions make it through the AMT calculation process, your minimum federal income tax payable for the year would be $8,424.00 or an effective rate of 8.4 percent. This increased tax of $1,493 ($8,424 − $6,931) represents a 21.7 percent increase in your tax bill for the year, compliments of the AMT requirement, driven by a formula that generally confuses 90 percent of the taxpaying public intentionally. You never see it coming until tax return preparation time; thus it is named the "stealth tax."

Some quick math will reveal that this AMT will be imposed on just about all taxpayers falling into the group that pays 80 percent (over 20 million households) of all federal personal income taxes collected.

HEALTH CARE—By definition, one of the meanings for the word "care" is watchful attention. Health care would presumably cover a person's attention to his or her individual health and well-being in several ways. For example, if we visit a doctor when we are not feeling well, exercise regularly, eat the proper foods and watch our diet, have annual physicals, refrain from smoking, too much drinking, or any conscious activity that would cause us physical harm, these are classic examples of health care as most of us would describe it.

HEALTH COVERAGE—This is a form of either private or publicly provided insurance that allows one to seek proper and immediate medical care for an illness or injury and not fear affordability or being bankrupted by the cost of the medical services provided. Private coverage is elective and generally available through a full range of health care insurance companies such as Aetna, Blue Cross, Blue Shield, Kaiser, United Health, Guardian, and many other entities for a fee. This coverage fee is either paid 100 percent by the individual who wants this type of insurance protection or shared between an employer and employee. Many people elect to not have such coverage, due to the prohibitive cost; this is the case for many millions of young people in their prime and in very good health. Many others who have no coverage at all can go into most hospitals in the country and receive emergency medical services, without charge; that is required by federal law. This is how low-income people of all ages and illegal immigrants obtain the medical care that they need.

If you listen carefully to our president and the political class, they always talk publicly about how many people, especially the children, are without "health coverage" and not "health care" that is in fact available to all (children, men, women, old, young, and illegal immigrants) for medical emergencies at thousands of hospitals around the country as a matter of federal law.

ARCTIC NATIONAL WILDLIFE REFUGE OR "ANWR"—An area within the state of Alaska containing more than 20 million acres of wilderness, uninhabited by human life, and in darkness six months each year. Approximately 1.5 million or 6 percent of the total acres represent the coastal plain area of the refuge. The coastal plain area has been the subject of much debate, as this is the area that the U.S. Geological Survey estimated to contain up to 5 billion barrels of recoverable oil. The United States currently consumes approximately 20 million barrels of oil per day, including all refined products such as motor fuel and so on. We import twelve million barrels on average per day and produce approximately 5 million from domestic sources, including offshore state and federal waters. If drilling commenced in the coastal plain area, they estimate daily production could reach a level of approximately 780,000 barrels per day or an increase over current domestic daily production of more than 15 percent. If you combine this increase with other alternative energy options such as wind, nuclear, and solar power, we certainly become significantly less dependent on foreign sources of energy in the form of crude oil.

CHAPTER 3

STATE-LEVEL OUT-OF-CONTROL SPENDING

The slowdown in our economy in 2008 and the crash of the financial markets will cause very severe problems for all states, but especially for the big-budget (spending) states such as New York, New Jersey, California, Massachusetts, Michigan, and Illinois, to name a few. Many of these states are, for the most part, heavily reliant on both income- and property-related taxes, but significant amounts are also raised from a host of other state-level and local taxes tied into the housing, banking, and finance industries. Plus, let us not forget to mention all those other nuisance taxes and other costs that may not be specifically labeled taxes, but really are a form of tax, as described below.

Has anyone noticed the cost to register a car has gone up dramatically in the past ten to fifteen years? How about your driver or other professional license renewal fees?

Have you gone to your local town hall recently for a permit of any kind, only to discover that the permit cost is now hundreds of dollars, rather than the $25 or $50 that the same permit cost just a few short years ago?

These are but a few of the many service or accommodation fees put in place by state and local governments that are not imposed as a tax, but nevertheless must be paid.

Now, back to some of the direct taxes we live with that are imposed by most states.

Real Estate Transfer and Mortgage Recording Taxes

All housing sales in New York (as well as many other states) are subject to some type of property transfer tax, generally payable at the closing. Many people don't focus on this transfer tax item at the closing, since there are so many forms to sign and so many numbers on the HUD statements; the tax is just accepted without question as a necessary part of the process. This house-transfer tax has generated many millions of dollars in revenue for the states each and every year for decades. Now that the housing industry is in a very deep slump, a good portion of this revenue stream has certainly dried up. In addition to this realty transfer tax, there is the mortgage recording tax. In New York, this mortgage recording tax is based upon the amount of your mortgage debt secured by property and may vary by county, but is in the range of fifty cents for each hundred dollars of debt.

To illustrate: If your mortgage was $400,000 at the time of closing, your mortgage recording tax cost would be $2,000 ($0.50 x $4,000). This is one of the elements that historically caused closing costs to be so high. In Connecticut, this particular recording tax is called the "real estate conveyance tax." In New Jersey, this tax is called the "realty transfer tax." Many other states do not have such a tax on the county recording of the mortgage obligation.

General Property Taxes

Taxes on real or personal property imposed by many states are usually assessed and collected locally by the counties, towns, and villages. This tax on land and structures on the land is the largest source of revenue for the state and local governments. The property taxes are fixed each year by the various levels of government within a state and are generally based on the full value of your property to meet most budget requirements. All the budgets generally include the cost of salaries paid for employees, including firemen, police, sanitation, schoolteachers, municipal workers, hospital workers, local road repair and maintenance personnel, taxing authority personnel, politician salaries, expenses, and so on. Also included are the pension costs for all the named groups of employees at the state, county, and local government agencies. More on this pension cost item a little later.

All the states provide some type of property tax relief program. Most of the programs are geared either to income level or age of the taxpayer; retirees with low incomes may be imposed upon to pay high property taxes that they simply cannot afford. Many states provide a homestead exemption that either exempts a certain amount of the home's value from property tax, grants credits that result in rebates, or allows deferral of tax until the property is sold. Some states have come up with a property tax swap, wherein property taxes are cut in exchange for increases in sales or other taxes. This last scheme is one to be cautious with, because it will never be a dollar-for-dollar exchange. To illustrate: the state of New Jersey increased the sales tax rate by 1 percent and gave half of the increase back in the form of property tax relief. What are you doing for me lately to get more taxes out of my hide?

The states also receive money from the federal government (actually they are distributing some of the total federal income taxes collected from residents of the state in the first place) to help the states support certain budget items and programs, especially those specifically mandated by the federal government. When the federal government cuts the amount of revenue they distribute to states, the states in turn cut their revenue distributions to the counties, cities, and towns in the state, and this creates a condition generally referred to as budget shortfalls.

As citizens, if we had budget shortfalls—meaning our expenses are higher than our income—we have two choices: 1) we cut our expenses and only spend what we have, or 2) we go into debt, using credit cards, borrowing from parents or other relatives, borrow on the equity in our homes or pension retirement savings or other resources that might be available. Regrettably, many of us choose to go into debt rather than forego a purchase of something we want or think we need now.

Looking back at the government budget shortfalls and how they trickle down to impact many of us in the form of invisible additional taxes that erode our disposable income, I found a classic example of how this trickle-down tax works. We received our annual mortgage escrow account history from the bank holding our mortgage in mid-October 2008, alerting me that my monthly mortgage payment would be going up due to an escrow shortage in our account. What this simply means is that my current monthly payment, which includes interest on my home loan, a small principal reduction, estimated property, school, and local taxes paid out by the bank to the county and city that I live in would be going up.. Specifically, the actual city tax went up a staggering 28.2 percent compared to the original bank projection, rising from $3,225.73 to $4,133.69. The school taxes went up 27.5 percent from $5,337.91 to $6,806.47, and the county taxes went up 25.6 percent from $2,876.39 to $3,613.94. What was most alarming to me was that the local newspapers had reported earlier in the year that all the tax categories would be going up, but at rates in the 5 to 7 percent range. My reaction to the outrageous tax increases was to call my local tax assessor's office and ask what was going on. The answer provided by a woman in the assessor's office was simple and readily available. "Yes, the school taxes were only expected to increase by 6.7 percent, but this increase assumed a certain amount of funding from the state. When the state reduces funding to the school districts throughout the state, the shortfall must be made up by passing it on to the homeowners." This is how the actual rate increased from a publicly reported 6.7 percent to 27.5 percent. I don't think many of the people in my town would have voted for such an increase, but they will have to accept it because that is the way the system is set up and currently operates. Please see a copy of the Escrow statement below received from the Wells Fargo Bank.

ESCROW ACCOUNT HISTORY

This is a review of the activity in your escrow account. It also compares our projections from your last review with the actual payments we made from your account.
Over this period, an additional $82.76 was deposited into your escrow account for interest on escrow.
An asterisk (*) indicates where a difference exists between your projected and actual account activity. The letter E beside an amount indicates that the payment or disbursement has not yet occurred, but is estimated to occur as shown. Payments are shown in the month received and not their month due. Please save this statement for comparison to your next analysis.
Please direct any questions to Customer Service at (800) 340-0473.

| | Payments to Escrow Account | | | Payments from Escrow Account | | | Escrow Account Balance | |
Month	Projected	Actual	Projected	Description	Actual		Projected	Actual
DEC/07	Beginning Balance						7,741.15	4,524.34
DEC/07	1,772.83	1,906.57 *	0.00		0.00		9,513.98	6,430.81
JAN/08	1,772.83	1,880.68 *	3,225.73	CITY TAX	4,133.69 *		8,061.08	4,177.90
JAN/08	0.00	0.00	4,496.00	HAZARD INS	0.00 *		3,565.08	4,177.90
FEB/08	1,772.83	1,880.68 *	0.00		0.00		5,337.91	6,058.58
MAR/08	1,772.83	1,908.02 *	0.00	HAZARD INS	2,529.00 *		7,110.74	5,437.60
APR/08	1,772.83	1,880.68 *	5,337.91	SCHOOL TAX	6,806.47 *		3,545.66	511.81
MAY/08	1,772.83	1,880.68 *	0.00		0.00		5,318.49	2,392.49
JUN/08	1,772.83	1,892.61 *	2,876.39	COUNTY TAXES	3,613.94 *		4,214.93	671.16
JUL/08	1,772.83	1,880.68 *	0.00		0.00		5,987.76	2,551.84
AUG/08	1,772.83	1,880.68 *	0.00		0.00		7,760.59	4,432.52
SEP/08	1,772.83	1,888.28 *	0.00		0.00		9,533.42	6,330.80
OCT/08	1,772.83	1,880.68 E	5,337.91	SCHOOL TAX	6,806.47 E		5,968.34	1,405.01
NOV/08	1,772.83	1,880.68 E	0.00		0.00 E		7,741.17	3,285.68

I asked the helpful woman in the tax office once again what was going on. She calmly stated that perhaps the total increase was for a period of more than a year, like eighteen or twenty-four months, since school taxes are paid each six months. But even if that were true, the rate increase is still astonishing, with most people having no recourse but to pay or get out of the state as soon as they can. An alternative never discussed at all is having the schools, counties, and cities cut expenses (using real cuts, not reductions in the rate of expenditure growth) rather than raise taxes. But the same old story is given out to the taxpayers as an excuse: we have to invest in our children, as they are the future; employer medical costs are increasing; state and local government employee salaries and other benefits are increasing; the stock market is down and nothing can be done to change any of these unfortunate circumstances.

More and more people are frustrated by these events and disagree that nothing can be done. Millions of others across the country in the big spend-and-tax states are likely arriving at the same conclusion very fast. Here is just a short list of actions that can and should be taken by local politicians in the big spending states in response to revenue shortfalls due to the economic slowdown and excesses of the past:

- Immediately eliminate all non-essential spending and programs, especially those programs that never should have been created in the first place.

- Freeze or cut the budgets of all departments. The cuts must be real and not just a cut in the rate of growth.

- Eliminate and hold the line on any wasteful spending.

- Have states that exclude all federal, state, and local government pension income from taxation cease this practice and tax the non-contributory portion as you would tax any other citizen in the state. After all, this pool of retirees is benefiting from all the services provided by the various government agencies, so why the free ride on income that was never before taxed? Many states exclude Social Security retirement benefits from state income taxes for good reason. Not less than half of Social Security benefits received represent the return of previously taxed income, and as such should not be taxed again. Only the employer portion of Social Security taxes paid on behalf of employees would represent untaxed income to the recipient. On this subject of Social Security benefits received, I need to point out that the returns we realize from our contributions over many years are far below what we would have realized had the funds been placed in the custody of more responsible and professional investment advisors in the private sector.

- Ensure that all children attending schools in the state are legally entitled to do so. If they are not because they are illegally in the country, send the bill for their attendance to the federal government until they figure out how to deal with all the extra taxpayer costs identified with illegal immigration. The same rules should apply for all health care and other related medical services provided by hospitals and physicians throughout many states in the United States. Please see chapter 5 for more on this subject.

- Put a cap on (or cut if necessary) all government and municipal salaries that have outpaced the private sector comparable salaries.

- Rope in pension costs by eliminating abuse and mismanagement of the municipal pension systems in place. For example, many municipal workers receive a retirement benefit that is based on the last three years of earnings, including overtime. In many instances, there is a silent, unspoken practice that municipal employees in the uniformed services category with several years to go on the job before retirement are loaded up with overtime, which in the majority of cases inflates annual pensions to the extent of an extra 50 to 100 percent of the base salary-driven pension benefit. Below, please review an excerpt from the *Journal News,* a local county newspaper (it does not matter which county, but rest assured the practice discussed here takes place in multiple counties in many states, all at taxpayer expense).

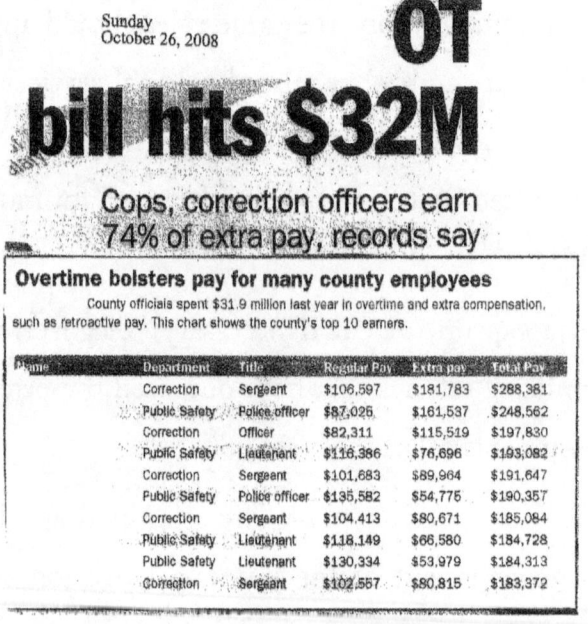

Sunday
October 26, 2008

OT bill hits $32M

Cops, correction officers earn 74% of extra pay, records say

Overtime bolsters pay for many county employees

County officials spent $31.9 million last year in overtime and extra compensation, such as retroactive pay. This chart shows the county's top 10 earners.

Name	Department	Title	Regular Pay	Extra pay	Total Pay
	Correction	Sergeant	$106,597	$181,783	$288,381
	Public Safety	Police officer	$87,025	$161,537	$248,562
	Correction	Officer	$82,311	$115,519	$197,830
	Public Safety	Lieutenant	$116,386	$76,696	$193,082
	Correction	Sergeant	$101,683	$89,964	$191,647
	Public Safety	Police officer	$135,582	$54,775	$190,357
	Correction	Sergeant	$104,413	$80,671	$185,084
	Public Safety	Lieutenant	$118,149	$66,580	$184,728
	Public Safety	Lieutenant	$130,334	$53,979	$184,313
	Correction	Sergeant	$102,557	$80,815	$183,372

Let's perform some simple and very understandable math on the reported overtime facts recited in the article. The chart above lists the ten county employees who earned the most money in overtime in the most recent fiscal year. This particular county has a combined workforce of 7,900 employees, with half earning some overtime at a cost of almost $32 million. That works out to an average of more than $8,000 in overtime for each worker logging overtime during the year. This average overtime cost amount is certainly not a lot when you consider that uniformed services personnel are on call for emergencies and by any measure reasonable. However, when you dig deeper into the details of the top OT earner, here is what we find.

Let's assume that the correction sergeant in this case earns an hourly rate of $51.25 based on a base pay of $106,597 per year. Using a standard 40-hour work week, the full year would equal 2,080 hours per year ($106,597 divided by 2,080 hours equals $51.25 per hour).

Let's further assume that all of his overtime was at time and one-half rates and further assuming that it is all related to overtime (only a small portion is likely related to the retroactive pay component made reference to in the article), divided by his hourly rate ($181,783 divided by $76.87 per hour overtime rate) works out to 2,364 hours of overtime worked in total at overtime rates.

What can we conclude from the above data? There are only 8,760 hours in each year, calculated by taking 24 hours per day multiplied by 365 total days in the year. That would mean this

Correction Sergeant worked a total of 4,444 hours for the year in total (2,080 regular hours plus 2,364 overtime hours) or 12.18 hours every single day, seven days a week. No holidays, no weekends off, no sick days, and no vacation. This I personally find incomprehensible. Now for the best part of this story. If our correction sergeant only earns half the amount of overtime ($181,783 divided by 2 = $90,090) for the next two years he is on the job and then retires, the combined salary and overtime pay per year become the basis for his pension calculation that may look something like this:

$288,381 for year one taken from the headline in the *Journal News,* $196,687 for years two and three ($106,597 base plus $90,090 in OT), gives us a three-year total of $681,755. This three-year total, divided by three representing the last three years of service on the job, works out to $227,252 average pay plus overtime earned per year.

Applying the pension formula that is generally used for uniformed services personnel (police, firemen, sanitation, transit workers, public safety officers, correction officers, and any others), the annual pension entitlement works out as follows, assuming twenty years of service:

$227,252 average of last three years' compensation multiplied by 20 (years of service actually worked/40 (maximum possible years actually worked) = $113,626 per year in pension benefits, free of state and local income taxes.

If our correction sergeant worked on this job for 30 years rather than 20, the pension benefit would be $170,439 per year ($227,252 x 30/40.) Now that's a pension benefit.

Referring back to the household income levels discussed in Chapter 2, this potential pension benefit amount is more than the amount of annual gross income earned by more than 80 percent of the households on their normal jobs before retiring. This illustration really has to sink in and be fully understood by everyone to grasp the magnitude of potential cost-related abuse going on all around the taxpayers in the area of public state and local pensions. The pension and other benefits related costs, such as free health care for life and excmption from all state and local pension income taxes, are the primary drivers of our tax increases year after year with no end in sight.Commitments to public-sector employees by our elected officials is totally out of control and finalized in closed door sessions without any input from the taxpayers footing the bill

Using only his normal base pay of $106,597 for each of the last three years on the job with no overtime pay and twenty years of service, our correction sergeant would receive a pension benefit of only $53,298, free of state and local income taxes. For thirty years of service, this annual pension amount increases to

$79,948. The pension amounts—while more modest absent the huge overtime component—are still much higher than the pre-retirement earnings of more than 50 percent of all households in the United States, and substantially greater than anything received for retirement by workers in the private sector who contribute all their working lives into a 401k retirement savings plan that may include some contribution from the employer. Employer-funded retirement plans enjoyed by federal, state, and local governments are a benefit of the past for just about all workers in the private sector.

A comparison of changes in pension benefits brought about by the overtime worked reveals the following:

Comparison Assuming 20 Years of Service for our Correction Sergeant

—Average Annual Compensation   <u>$227,252</u>
(last three years of service per above)

—Annual Calculated Pension Benefit $113,626
(including OT pay assumptions per above)

—Normal Annual Pension Benefit
(assuming no OT pay earned in last three years)   <u>$ 53,298</u>

Resulting Annual Increase over Normal Pension   <u>$ 60,328</u>

Percent Change in Annual Pension Benefit   113 percent

Comparison Assuming 30 Years of Service for our Correction Sergeant

—Average Annual Compensation $227,252
(last three years of service per above)

—Annual Calculated Pension Benefit $170,439
(including OT pay assumptions per above)

—Normal Annual Pension Benefit
(assuming no OT pay earned in last three years) $ 53,298

Resulting Annual Increase over Normal Pension $ 117,141

Percent Change in Annual Pension Benefit   220 percent

So again I ask who pays all the extra pension costs.

State and local taxpayers do, of course, as part of all the different taxes collected during the year to cover the state and local budget expenditures that include a portion of the pension cost contributions for municipal employee pensions. The portion of pension money funded each year by the state and local governments is placed in pension fund trusts and invested by professional investment firms.

The pension funds earn money (see additional comments further on below on New York City pension funds and investment returns) in the form of interest, dividends, and capital gains from the investing activities. The million-dollar question, of course, is whether the investing activities cover the total pension obligations. If the stock market and economy are thriving, no annual contributions by the state and local governments may be required. If the stock market and economy are faltering, the additional contributions required to cover the estimated pension liabilities can be crippling. In fact, due to the poorly performing financial markets in the past two years or so and the stock market collapse in late 2008, many states will see their outlays for pension costs rise dramatically. In New York, the total of pension cost contributions to all plans was less than 10 percent of the total state budgeted expenses. The projected contribution required for the year 2008 was expected to increase to a level of approximately 16 percent of the total budgeted expenses (perhaps even more now due to the recent stock market crash in the late summer of 2008) with additional increases above the 16 percent level for the foreseeable future. The incremental pension contributions are a principal driver, causing the large deficits forecasted due to the collapse of the financial markets in the state of New York. California, New Jersey, Illinois, Michigan, and many other states and local governments share a similar fate, with no relief in sight. This forecasted deficit problem caused the governors of the large spend states to recently visit Washington, DC, to beg for money needed to cover the shortfalls in their budgets because they dread facing the reality of having to increase taxes of every type, cutting services, and so on. Regrettably, many of the very generous municipal employee contracts entered into by our past and present elected officials with state and local workers cannot be undone, and therefore, there is not much they can do to reduce these costs at this time. Having said that, something certainly can be done about longer-term future costs and the abuses inherent in the current system, especially in the area of pension and other benefits covering municipal employees (currently active or retired).

The majority of people, in my opinion, sincerely believe that most municipal employees have worked admirably for many years, earning their pension and other benefits. I personally (and many other taxpayers, I am sure) don't have a problem with funding the normal pension cost that our taxes are designed to pay for. This is especially true for the brave first responders and other public-sector employees who serve the thousands of communities in the United States; we all take comfort in knowing that they are there for us. The issue and complaint present here is why do we have to pay for unchecked abusive and out-of-control practices that increase the cost of many individual pensions twofold or more?

My proposed solution to limit the pension abuses described above would require that no single employee should be able to retire on a pension that exceeds 20 percent of his or her normal pension based on an average base salary of the last three or five years, excluding overtime. Applying this solution to our Correction Sergeant would result in his receiving a normal pension of $53,298 and a maximum possible pension of $63,958 (120 percent of the normal pension). Additionally, his pension should be fully taxable at the state and local level, since while the good sergeant dedicated his twenty or thirty years to public service, he was well compensated and granted security for life in the form of his pension and other retirement benefits, such as health care; plus, he benefits from all the state services provided and paid for by the private-sector taxpaying residents of the state. Again, this illustrative pension amount is substantially more than most people get in the private sector, if anything at all, and a great burden on all taxpayers in the state.

Municipal workers' unions should have no objections to this proposed amended pension formula with a cap set at 120 percent if the allegation of overtime abuse (and disability pension abuses as well) in arriving at pension entitlements is not true. Regrettably, in many states, taxpayers will sooner or later discover that this pension overtime (or disability pension) scam just before retirement is indeed true, and the reaction to such a proposal by certain union representatives of the municipal workers will be nothing less than hostile outrage. The sad part of this truth is that in order for our state legislators to remain in the good graces of the municipal workers' unions to whom they are beholden, the tab will continue to be paid by all other taxpayers in the various large-spending states. The big question is when and at what level of cost to the genuine taxpaying public does this pension excess stop?

In support of my comments above on the excess taxpayer cost of pension and other retiree benefits to municipal workers, a local Westchester newspaper reported that the secrecy about the details of new commitments contained in proposed contracts with public employee unions until they are ratified is costing taxpayers millions of dollars in the form of property and other local taxes necessary to fund the new costs. This is not a problem unique to New York, but rather a widespread practice in many states. A watchdog group in New York named Empire Center for New York State Policy is proposing that taxpayers be informed before final commitments are made to any public employee union by their elected legislative representatives, the cost of which will find its way into the taxes paid by them. Once the commitments negotiated are finalized, it is too late for them to be debated or altered." A list of contracts negotiated in secrecy was also provided in the news article that included a Johnson City, New York contract providing for a 44 percent raise over a five-year period, or three times the current annual rate of inflation, while we are heading into a severe global recession. Several other contracts were cited, but officials refused to disclose details to the people who will pay the tab.

Remember, many big-spend states are looking at billions of dollars in revenue shortfalls due to the slowdown in the economy and unchecked spending increases over many years. Any cuts in state-level (all states, to be clear) aid to school districts within the individual states will certainly result in higher (very likely significantly higher) local property taxes if expenditures are not cut to match the cuts in lost state aid.

Why? Just think about the cumulative increases in spending over the years that cause expenses to become fixed and inescapable. My current year property tax increase experience, made reference to elsewhere in this chapter, is only the beginning of what we are all in for, especially since my increase was imposed before any of the big revenue shortfall problems in many states even hit the headlines.

Pension and health care benefits reform for municipal employees in many of the larger states and cities throughout the country is desperately needed before taxpayers footing the bill are burdened to the point where the entire services system collapses under the pressure of ever-increasing, unaffordable taxation.

Sales and Use Taxes, Including Gross Receipts Taxes

Just about everything we buy except food is subject to a sales-type tax imposed by many states and local governments. This sales-type tax is on the final sale of product and totally independent of other additional taxes that we are required to pay on specific items that I will list immediately following the Sales and Use Taxes section.

Believe it or not, there are only five states that currently do not impose general statewide sales and use tax: Alaska, Delaware, Montana, New Hampshire, and Oregon.

The current 2008 rates at the state level alone range from a low of 2.9 percent in Colorado to a high of 7 percent for New Jersey, Rhode Island, and Tennessee. In the case of Rhode Island, as well as Connecticut, Indiana, Maine, Maryland, Massachusetts, Michigan, Mississippi, West Virginia, and Washington, DC, local sales and use taxes are not authorized on all but a limited number of transactions, such as perhaps the purchase of a car or boat.

Numerous other states such as California, Florida, Illinois, Minnesota, Nevada, New Jersey, Pennsylvania, South Carolina, Tennessee, Texas, Vermont, and Washington have their rates set in the range of 6 to 7 percent, but keep in mind that additional sales and use taxes can also be imposed at the county and local level as well. While New York is noticeably absent from this list covering states in the 6 to 7 percent range (the state rate is currently only 4 percent), counties and cities throughout the state add their levy, bringing the average combined sales and use tax rates to 8.75 percent. That's correct: $8.75 for every $100 spent in New York City (and many other nearby counties and cities) out of your disposable income is for sales taxes. Please see chapter 2 for the definition of "disposable income." The same condition can be found in California, New Jersey, Illinois, and multiple other states. Please keep in mind that Florida, Nevada, and Texas are states that do not impose a personal income tax on their residents.

State Inheritance and Estate Taxes

If someone such as a parent, loved one, or friend dies and leaves you an inheritance of some kind, you will have a state inheritance tax to pay. Eleven states collect this tax including Connecticut, Indiana, Iowa, Kansas, Kentucky, Maryland, Nebraska, New Jersey and Oregon.

Estate taxes are imposed on estates left by a person who dies. Currently, the federal government has an estate tax that is scheduled to be completely repealed in 2010, but I don't think it is going to happen. Additionally, seventeen states also have an estate tax that is in some way tied to the federal estate tax, but they have changed their respective estate tax regulations to avoid the loss of revenue caused by federal level estate tax credits. The seventeen states include Illinois, Kansas, Maine, Maryland, Massachusetts, Minnesota, New Jersey, New York, North Carolina, Ohio, Oregon, Rhode Island, Vermont, Virginia, Wisconsin, Nebraska and Washington. In addition, Washington D.C. also imposes this tax as well.

Specific Additional Taxes

Specific taxes we all pay in most states are in addition to the sales and use taxes. These are imposed mostly on companies that pass them on to us and embedded in the price of the items we buy. It increases their final cost at the retail level, where we make the final purchases. These taxes include:

Alcohol Tax—Tax we pay each time we purchase beer, wine, and hard liquor in establishments other than bars and restaurants for home consumption.

Fuel Tax—Generally a tax we pay with our purchase of gasoline at the pump. We also pay this incremental tax when we pay for our heating oil or gas, purchase of airline tickets, transportation of goods we buy that are delivered by common carriers and the like, and just about all products that have some element of fuel or petroleum.

Tobacco Tax—Tax we pay on packs of cigarettes, cigars, and pipe and chewing tobacco.

Parking Tax—Every time you park at a private garage in a major city, you are subject to this tax. In New York City, the rate is 18 percent or more.

Hotel Occupancy Tax—Tax we pay for each night we lodge at a hotel. The rates are usually 15 percent or more.

Leased Vehicles Gross Receipts Tax—A tax we pay in certain states where we rent a car or other vehicle.

Severance Taxes—Paid to certain natural resource extraction states and/or counties on the value of produced oil, natural gas, natural gas liquids, most non-metallic minerals, coal, and timber, to name the most significant well-known products. Incidentally, in case you were not aware, New York, California, Pennsylvania, Ohio, and Michigan are among the natural resource-producing states with oil, natural gas, natural gas liquids production, and so on. Most people only think of Texas, Wyoming, Oklahoma, Louisiana, Mississippi, and New Mexico as the more prominently known oil- and gas-producing states, but there are many others.

Telecommunications Taxes—Paid for line access, telephones, and other telecommunications devices.

<u>Utilities Taxes</u>—Paid by the utility companies in some states for the privilege of operating a public utility.

The above is by no means an all-inclusive list of the taxes imposed on business that are passed on to all of us as consumers, but I thought putting together this abbreviated listing was important to understand the broad reach of the indirect taxes we pay every day.

Many of the big-spending states, and unfortunately their residents, are in big trouble due to the consistent reckless and irresponsible spending by state legislatures across the country. A good portion of the annual spending increases is related to municipal unions and patronage, pet projects, and let's not forget the embedded systemic corruption, especially in the area of pensions.

States in deep trouble include New York, New Jersey, Connecticut, California, Michigan, Illinois, Wisconsin, and Maryland. All have had to increase taxes across the board significantly. Many of these states require workers to join unions, and therefore the employment growth is much lower than in states that do not have such a requirement.

Clearly the state-level income taxes produce the second-largest revenue stream for the respective states, after property taxes. There are state-level corporate income taxes and state-level individual personal income taxes.

In 2008, forty-six states and the District of Columbia imposed corporate income taxes for the privilege of doing business in the respective states, and forty-four states and Washington, DC imposed individual personal income taxes for the privilege of living in a particular state.

Which six states (as of November 2008) do not impose income taxes on individuals?

Florida

Nevada

North Dakota

South Dakota

Texas

Wyoming

New Hampshire and Tennessee only impose income taxes on dividends and interest, but not wages and other sources of individual income.

Many of us know or have heard how confusing and complex our current income-taxing system is to understand for many taxpayers. One of the contributing factors to this complexity is that many states treat items of income differently from the federal income tax treatment. Why? In most instances, to raise more revenue and not make it part of the tax rates imposed on income, as this is politically incorrect and therefore unacceptable. What is really happening to taxpayers is simple. Eliminating tax deductions raises our tax bill without the tax rate changing. This maneuver allows the politicians to claim they have not increased tax rates.

For example, let us assume that a particular state's income tax rate is 5 percent. If your gross income was $150 and your state taxable income after allowing all the same federal deductions is $100, your state income tax would simply be $5. On the other hand, if the state in this example does not allow the same federal income tax deduction for interest paid on your mortgage, your federal deductions get adjusted downward from $100 to $90 by the state formula; in this instance, that effectively increases your state taxable income from $100 to $110. At the 5 percent income tax rate, your state income tax bill jumps from $5 to $5.50, a 10 percent increase. At the same time, the state income tax rate of 5 percent does not increase, but your tax bill *did* increase. These are the political games that confuse people, and the reason why so many people are fleeing the high spend-and-tax states like California and New York. Many years ago, there was a local radio show in the New York City tri-state area named "Talk to the Governor." One retired caller said he was born in New York, worked and lived there all of his life, but now as a retired person had to leave because the tax burden was too high and he could not afford essential items on his meager pension. The then-governor responded, "We have not raised the tax rate for several years, and in fact reduced it two years ago." The caller was speechless and did not know how to respond about the games of disallowing certain deductions, as he was not a tax professional. And of course, the governor sounded like such a nice guy, telling the half-truth. True, while the state income tax rates may not have changed, deductions were likely disallowed, with actual taxes paid going up. Moreover, if the state cut aid during this period to the school districts or counties in the state, local property taxes would have increased to cover the shortfall, and everyone's combined tax burden would surly have increased without a change in any of the tax rates on income, property, or sales. In this way, our esteemed elected representatives at every level of government can boast that they held the line on tax rates but not on the amount of absolute total tax dollars paid in a given year.

For example, in 2008, eight states did not use the federal income amount for taxing, but some other base. Twelve states did not offer a standard deduction. Certain states disallowed certain federal-level deductions from gross income and partially allowed others. Many credits granted at the federal level were also completely or partially disallowed.

A recent study conducted by the American Legislative Exchange Council *(www.alec.org)* revealed that over the past ten years, the ten states with the most spending and highest taxes had only half the population and job growth, compared to the ten states with the least economic burden. Moreover, the big-spending high-tax states also experienced substantially lower growth in income. What this all means in a nutshell is that new jobs are being created at a substantially greater rate in states with lower taxes and less spending, making the business environment more attractive and competitive. Texas and Florida are two of the nine states with no income taxes in place, and they are significantly outperforming large-spending states like New York and California in the areas of job growth. This is attracting both corporations and new households fleeing from the big-spend states in large numbers.

The flight of corporations and households from the northeastern states started in the late '60s and early '70s, when many of the major oil companies left New York State (with headquarters buildings in New York City) due to the imposition of high corporate income taxes. Most, if not all, of these entities went to Texas, where they not only avoided the income taxes but also found the Texas business regulatory environment much less onerous and overall the most cost efficient to operate in. The oil companies were followed by many other entities, and the flight again included many of the households working for these companies as well. While the United States continues to create manufacturing jobs, this job growth is being realized in the South rather than the Northeast and California, due to the high taxes, higher labor cost, and expensive regulatory compliance.

Taxpayers in many of the big-spend states are fed up and frustrated with the constant ever-increasing tax burdens that will no doubt worsen in 2009 and beyond as we will have trillions of dollars in new federal debt to service. This will push taxpayers more and more in the direction of a tax revolt of some kind.

The state of Michigan has been having a very difficult time getting through their weakened local economy, primarily driven by persistent problems plaguing the auto industry.

The revenue shortfall for fiscal year 2009 in that state is estimated to be in the $500 million range. This shortfall comes on the heels of very large income tax increases last year that were in the range of 11.5 percent. The idea of the increase was to raise more than a billion dollars in new tax revenues that would be used to stimulate Michigan's weak economy. Several months into the new 2008 tax year, the expected revenues were well below projections, and the statewide recession persisted. The tax increases, rather than increasing state revenues, have prompted many families and businesses to actually leave the state, seeking to avoid the new taxes altogether. Additionally, property taxes are rising despite declining home values. Taxpayers must ask why the elected officials in the state of Michigan do not cut state spending or eliminate waste and abuse as an alternative to increased taxes.

In Massachusetts, there was a ballot measure in 2008 to abolish the state's income tax. If this ballot was successful on Election Day, it could have wiped out $12 billion of revenue, which would have paralyzed the entire state, since it has a total budget of $28 billion per year.

North Dakota also had a ballot measure in 2008 calling for a 50 percent reduction in state income tax rates and a 15 percent reduction in the corporate income tax rate.

Maine, Oregon, and Arizona also had tax-reduction initiatives on the 2008 ballot.

In my opinion, the tax initiatives appearing are only the beginning of what I view as a taxpayer uprising in the making.

California is facing a budget deficit of more than $40 billion over the next two years. Budget reform and spending controls were promised by the governor back in 2003, but nothing was ever done. In the last four years alone, the budget in our most-populated state has grown by 40 percent, and now the state is looking to increase their sales tax rate by 1.5 percent to 9.25 percent for many counties in California, at a time when all retailers are experiencing a severe slowdown in sales.

The Democratic-controlled state legislature refuses to trim the budget. California's problems stem from out-of-control spending by the state's elected representatives and the massive dollar drain on services provided to illegal immigrants, and not from a shortage of tax dollars flowing into the state treasury.

In New York, the new governor has been battling with the state legislators about what is needed for the state to address the fiscal crisis it finds itself in. State revenues are quickly declining, due to the problems on Wall Street, as New York City is the financial capital of the world. The forecasted state deficits are growing, jobs are disappearing, unemployment in the private sector is rising, and higher taxes are driving households and businesses out of the state in record numbers. As of October 2008, New York State is now estimating a deficit of up to $15 billion for 2009 and a $42.5 billion deficit over the years 2009 to 2012, mostly caused by the problems in the financial sector of the economy, combining with many expensive social spending programs.

Despite the appeals from the governor to substantially cut the 2009 budget, the *New York Post* reported that the state legislators are ready to hand the unions big benefits windfalls that can cost taxpayers in the state many millions of dollars each year in the future. This is why the teachers' union president in New York City objected to putting a cap on the annual increases in the property tax, because she knows this is where the funds to cover the out-of-control schools cost and spending mostly come from. Guess what? The New York legislators failed to support the proposed cap on the property taxes, delivering a major victory to the teachers' union while serving another blow to the head of Joe the Taxpayer.

Some other bills being considered by the state legislators in New York State, as reported the New York Post in the summer of 2008 include a bill to make it impossible for state and local governments to not cut health benefits for public-sector retirees, even if the state finds itself in a severe budget crisis. This would never be permitted in the private sector. Another bill would lower retirement ages and boost pension benefits for various categories of public employees, costing hundreds of millions of dollars in the future over and above the current level of expenses. These are just two examples of how the legislators cater to and take care of the unions that support them with millions of dollars in political action committee (PAC) contributions, most from union dues collected, with the remaining taxpayers in the state footing the bill for all the extravagant benefits programs that ensure a virtually unencumbered retirement for civil servants. I have no issue with reasonable, competitive, and normal benefits programs awarded to civil servants. The problem we face is that the costs for such programs are financially out of control. Very few citizens are aware of the details that keep driving our taxes up consistently year after year. Again, the key question is where and when does this escalation process end?

The dilemma facing taxpayers now and over the next twenty years or so is the impact of the recent stock market collapse on state pension funds. As reported by Bloomberg Financial News on January 13, 2009, "state governments from Rhode Island to California have run up estimated pension losses of $865.1 billion," a decline of 37 percent for the 14-month period ending December 16, 2008. This loss exceeds the $700 billion bailout program approved by Congress in October 2008.

The amount of loss is so huge that even if markets recover, the bulk of it will have to be made up in the future by taxpayers.

Wow! Not only does Joe the Taxpayer get stuck with the extravagant basic pension cost to begin with, he now gets stuck with paying the tab for the market losses suffered by the pension fund as well.

By the way, in the same Bloomberg Financial News flash disclosing the $865.1 million in state pension fund losses, the article also reported the following:

"Excluding Social Security, public employers' pension costs are three times the retirement costs of their private counterparts, according to a June 2008 report by the

Washington-based Employee Benefit Research Institute."
(www.EBRI.org)

The biggest problem with states like New York, New Jersey, California, Illinois, and Michigan that I cannot emphasize enough is that the state legislators simply commit to spend ever-increasing amounts of money, which will not be available without tax increases, to secure the favor and support of the various public-sector unions when the legislators seek re-election. This practice has gone on for too many years and they simply refuse to stop it.

To illustrate how long the excessive spending has been going on in New York, I have inserted below a *New York Post article* dated Tuesday, August 2, 1994 that so astonished me at that time, I could not discard it. The article is self-explanatory in terms of how benefits programs were very unfair to working New Yorkers, but how many of us really believe that the benefits amounts have gone down since 1994 rather than up? Keep in mind that more than 50 percent of the working households in 2007 earned less than $50,000 per year, so something is dreadfully wrong with the system in place that penalizes working households through higher tax burdens and rewards those households that don't work. I hasten to add that there are indeed families, households, and individuals throughout the country that need assistance, but this assistance must be reasonable, balanced, and affordable when measured against other existing economic realities.

Separately, please note in the 1994 article that there is also a list of starting salaries for municipal jobs at that time. Please take a moment to compare this list to the facts recited below in a more recent *New York Post* editorial published in late 2008 dealing with cost of public-sector salaries and benefits in states where the current cost of fringe benefits averaged $38,000 per year for each city worker. This amount substantially exceeds every starting salary on the 1994 article listing that puts all of the ever-increasing spending by city and state (and federal) governments into perspective.

NEW YORK POST, TUESDAY, AUGUST 2, 1994

Workers must earn 45G a year to match welfare recipients

By FREDRIC DICKER
State Editor

ALBANY — Working New Yorkers must earn nearly $45,000 a year to get the same benefits given many welfare recipients, a conservative anti-tax group said yesterday.

"It is often said that New York provides a Cadillac-style welfare program. Rolls Royce is more like it," charged Change-NY President Tom Carroll.

The group made public a study showing an average New York City single mother with two children on welfare — "a typical recipient" — receives non-taxable city, state and federal benefits of $32,571.

That's the equivalent of a $44,900 annual salary before taxes, Change-NY said.

The group said the $32,571 figure is "extremely conservative" because it excluded the value of other benefits such as Head Start, job training, child care, and the Special Supplemental Food program for Women, Infants and Children (WIC).

But State Social Services Department spokeswoman Deborah Adler called Change-NY's assertions "fiction, not fact."

She said the group's calculations "would not apply to the vast majority of Aid to Families with Dependent Children (ADC) cases since almost no one would be eligible for all the benefits included in the 'typical' case."

Adler said the actual per-year cost for a mother on welfare was about $14,003 and not $32,571.

Change-NY stood by its figures, and accused the Social Services Department of low-balling actual costs.

The biggest points of contention between the two sides were Medicaid and housing costs — which Change-NY said were $15,000 higher than the state's estimates.

Change-NY called New York's welfare payments "an incredible disincentive for welfare recipients to make the transition from welfare to work.

"After all, why accept a job that requires 40 hours of work a week when you can remain at home and make the equivalent of $44,900 annually?"

New York's welfare payments topped the starting salaries of a wide range of Big Apple municipal workers including office aides ($17,675), teachers ($26,903), police officers ($27,155) and housing inspectors ($28,490).

The group also noted that sending welfare recipients to Harvard would be cheaper than New York's current approach.

State welfare records show 1,263,644 mothers and children receive Aid to Families with Dependent Children and another 396,191 individuals receive home relief.

Welfare benefits in N.Y. State*	
Assistance program	Annual amount
Basic cash grant	$ 2,856
Medicaid	13,664
Housing assistance	9,828
Food assistance	4,507
Energy assistance	1,716
TOTAL	**32,571**
Pre-tax equivalent of welfare benefit level	44,900

*Benefit level for a woman with two children. Source: Change NY

Starting salaries: municipal jobs	
Graduate field	Starting salary
Office aide	$17,675
Word processor	18,272
Sanitation worker	23,104
Correction officer	25,977
Teacher	26,903
Police officer	27,155
Firefighter	27,155
Housing inspector	28,490
Ferry deckhand	30,942

Source: City Hall

In early November 2008, New York's governor presented his proposals to close the gap in the budget, which included a possible renegotiation of public employee union contracts. The union leaders simply ignored the request by asking *what is in it for us?* Many people in the state are unaware that the 200,000-plus state employees have an annual average salary in 2008 of $86,000. If you include irrevocable pensions and increased annual benefits, this figure will rise to $92,000 per employee by 2010. The total annual payroll cost for this pool of state personnel is more than $17 billion or approximately 15 percent of the state budget for the year. This amount is in addition to $20 billion in state aid to the schools that largely fund teachers' salaries; keep in mind that overall compensation to teachers is equally rewarding, in addition to the generous pensions that are not subject to New York income taxes, even though the public employees benefit from all the state-provided services.

New York City also has a problem with the high cost of public employees, as highlighted in the January 12, 2009 *New York Post* editorial also inserted below:

Time To Chop Jobs

A new report on the cost of New York City employees suggests strongly that layoffs may be unavoidable.

Let's face it: City Hall is growing broker and broker. Personnel expenses are burgeoning, yet little can be done about it in the short term — aside from chopping jobs.

The report — an invaluable contribution by the Citizens Budget Commission — shows just how out of control these costs have become.

Are you sitting down?

● The hit for an average firefighter, counting pay and benefits, is an eye-popping *$186,464 a year.*

● A cop costs $164,045.

● Average city employees run "only" $107,000 each, with some $38,000 of that for fringe benefits.

But the scariest part is how *fast* these costs have grown: In 2000 — shortly before Mike Bloomberg became mayor — the city's yearly tab was just $65,000 per average employee. So the cost has soared fully *63 percent* since then — *twice as fast* as in the private sector.

Most telling: Fringe benefits have nearly tripled — from $13,000 to $38,000 a year. Pension costs, in particular, are up a mind-numbing *700 percent* — from $2,530 a head to $20,333.

The timing couldn't be worse: The In-dependent Budget Office says the city is slated to overspend revenues next year by $4.3 billion — and *$7 billion* the year after that.

And since City Hall, unlike the feds, can't print money, options are limited.

Certainly, pensions need to be contained. But that's largely up to the union-bought state Legislature — so don't count on it. (Reforms wouldn't likely kick in soon enough, anyway.)

Municipal employees should also be made to chip in for their health care — as most private employees do.

And city salaries, which have outpaced inflation, need to be frozen, if not *cut.*

Even so, with these out-of-the-ballpark personnel costs, Bloomberg & Co. will have no choice but to shed bodies.

Rolling back the head count to the level of eight years ago would mean nearly 7,000 fewer staffers. At $107,000 a head, that translates to savings of more than $700 million a year.

Here's the bottom line: Public employees live in the same world as everyone else — a world in which pricey pay packages increasingly mean layoffs and workers must sacrifice to save jobs.

Unless city unions step up and offer dramatic givebacks (i.e., unless hell freezes over), pink slips are inevitable.

So be it.

NY POST 1/12/09

Data released by the Census Bureau in 2008 indicated that state and local tax collections in New York State for fiscal year 2005 were $1.1 trillion, 8.5 percent higher than fiscal year 2004, or 2.5 times the rate of inflation for that year. This increase in state and local tax collections is directly attributed to the Bush tax cuts that provided much more disposable income and thus fueled spending that brought the higher taxes into the state coffers. New York was the top tax state at the time (Connecticut was runner-up) with a combined state and local tax burden per person of $5,770. This figure was 56 percent above the national average. One would think that New York taxpayers were in for some property, income, or other tax cuts in the 2006 year that followed, given this huge windfall by the state. But this was pure fantasy, as it would have required holding the line on spending that is simply not possible in any year for the politicians who run things in Albany (and most other large-spend states as well). Instead, the proposed budget for the 2006 year in New York contained a 6.3 percent spending increase, with most of the increases earmarked for health care and schools, including salaries and pension costs. In fact, it would have been prudent to hold some of this 2005 revenue windfall in reserve, so that if we experienced a slowdown in the economy, there would be no need to increase taxes when things in the economy were weakening. Does this not make sense to anyone running things? New York politicians would argue that the increases in spending are caused by federal cuts and mandates. But this was certainly not the case, since the federal treasury was itself loaded with higher tax collections that had increased revenue into the federal treasury by more than 16 percent in the first full year that the Bush tax cuts were kicking in.

Looking down one level in New York State to New York City (where there is a very capable and well-respected businessman/mayor in place running that city), in late October 2008, the local newspapers reported that a certain amount (approximately 3 percent of $39 billion) of the New York City Employee Retirement System pension funds was placed in risky hedge funds during the height of the Wall Street financial collapse. Hedge funds are unregulated entities with large buckets of cash assets that invest in a wide assortment of investments. They seek higher rewards than normal conservative investing would yield and therefore can be risky. A worldwide hedge fund research group reported that hedge funds on average lost 20 percent of their value for the ten-month period ending October 31, 2008. This decline has caused investors to bail out due to the high risks, and this exodus causes the overall value of the hedge fund to decline as well. Some additional facts also reported in the news revealed that:

- The five New York City pension funds had $105 billion in assets as of June 30, 2008.

- Losses for the year through September 30, 2008 were in the range of $8.8 billion, or 8.5 percent, and this is before the market collapse in October 2008.

- Investment management fees expected to be paid in 2009 are in the range of $132 million, up from $29 million paid in 2003. Admittedly, we need professionals managing these assets, but the bulk of fees should be performance-driven and paid only when assets appreciate and not when they depreciate. After all, the taxpayer ultimately pays the fees when investment earnings are down; additional contributions are needed to make up shortfalls required to fund the estimated pension liabilities in total.

• Over the next three years, New York City will contribute an estimated $26.5 billion to cover shortfalls in pension-cost estimates that cover 250,000 retirees and 350,000 active city workers. This is over and above the very limited contributions made to the pension funds by employees.

Unfortunately, these reported statistical facts on New York City also apply to many other large cities and states throughout the country. This is probably the reason why many states had ballot proposals on Election Day 2008 to substantially reduce income taxes and provide some form of tax relief to the taxpayers.

2, 2008   nypost.com

■ **$104.7 BILLION** in all five city pension funds as of June 30.

■ **$8.8 BILLION** in losses (8.5%) through Sept. 30.

■ **237,000** retired city workers or their beneficiaries draw pensions.

■ **344,000** city workers are paying into the NYCERS system.

■ **$132 MILLION** budgeted by NYCERS for investment management fees in FY 2009 — up from $29 million in 2003.

■ **$26.7 BILLION** in taxpayer funds will be paid by the city in the next 3 years to cover shortfalls in pension contribution costs.

■ **20%** losses were recorded through Oct. 29 in a worldwide index of hedge funds tracked by Chicago-based Hedge Fund Research Inc.

In closing this chapter covering the state and local tax picture, below is a list of all fifty states, reflecting the state and local tax burden as a percentage of household income for fiscal year 2008. The problem we face going into the 2009 calendar year as taxpayers is the biggest recession upon us since the 1930s. Declining tax-revenue collections in all states due to the slowdown in the economy, combined with cuts in federal funds flowing to the states and substantially higher unemployment, will likely bring about state and local tax increases in just about every possible category available and discussed in this chapter.

How states rank

Combined state-local tax burden as a percentage of average household income for fiscal year 2008:

Rank, state	Tax burden	Rank, state	Tax burden	Rank, state	Tax burden	Rank, state	Tax burden
1. N.J.	11.8%	15. Maine	10.0%	29. W.Va.	9.3%	43. Texas	8.4%
2. N.Y.	11.7%	16. Ga.	9.9%	30. Ill.	9.3%	44. Tenn.	8.3%
3. Conn.	11.1%	17. Neb.	9.8%	31. Iowa	9.3%	45. S.D.	7.9%
4. Md.	10.8%	18. Va.	9.8%	32. Mo.	9.2%	46. N.H.	7.6%
5. Hawaii	10.6%	19. Okla.	9.8%	33. N.D.	9.2%	47. Fla.	7.4%
6. Calif.	10.5%	20. N.C.	9.8%	34. Colo.	9.0%	48. Wyo.	7.0%
7. Ohio	10.4%	21. Kan.	9.6%	35. Wash.	8.9%	49. Nev.	6.6%
8. Vt.	10.3%	22. Utah	9.6%	36. Miss.	8.9%	50. Alaska	6.4%
9. Wis.	10.2%	23. Mass.	9.5%	37. S.C.	8.8%	U.S. average	9.7%
10. R.I.	10.2%	24. Del.	9.5%	38. Ala.	8.6%		
11. Pa.	10.2%	25. Ky.	9.4%	39. N.M.	8.6%		
12. Minn.	10.2%	26. Ore.	9.4%	40. Mont.	8.6%		
13. Idaho	10.1%	27. Mich.	9.4%	41. Ariz.	8.5%		
14. Ark.	10.0%	28. Ind.	9.4%	42. La.	8.4%		

Note: Percentages are rounded, causing some states with same tax burden to have different rank.
Source: Tax Foundation

CHAPTER 4

WONDERFUL WORLD OF U.S. FEDERAL TAXES

Did you know that the Internal Revenue Code, the document with all the rules and regulations governing federal taxes, contains more than 3.5 million words? How many words is that? They would fill up 7,500 letter-size pages each containing 60 lines per page. That's a lot of words indeed. Just think about what the average politician can do with such a treasury of words that make up our complex tax regulations. When they talk to their constituents about how they will reduce taxes or promise to tax the rich or wealthy if elected and provide relief to the middle class, most of their words do not even appear among the 3.5 million words.

Can you imagine what a nightmare it would be for the average person looking for something buried in this huge document?

For the obvious reasons recited above, and in the interest of trying to explain in simple lay terms, some very important aspects of our federal tax policies and regulations that we all need to understand, this chapter will be devoted to broad areas of federal taxation that we encounter in our everyday lives, either by listening to the radio, reading a news article, preparing our income tax returns, or listening to a speech given by a politician. In chapter 2, I provided certain definitions in the hope that we have some basic understanding of certain very relevant terms and their true meaning.

The 3.5 million words cover the following areas referred to in the Internal Revenue Code as subtitles:

- Income Taxes

- Estate and Gift Taxes

- Employment Taxes

- Miscellaneous Excise Taxes

- Alcohol, Tobacco, and Certain Other Excise Taxes

- Procedure and Administration

- The Joint Committee on Taxation

- Financing of Presidential Election Campaigns

- Trust Fund Code

- Coal Industry Health Benefits

- Group Health Plan Requirements

Let's start at the top of the pyramid in attempting to understand what takes place in terms of how income tax rules, rates, and other related areas of taxation become an integral part of our lives as U.S. citizens.

In an earlier chapter, reference was made to the "Bush tax cuts." I need to be perfectly clear here, so everyone understands that no president ever imposed or cut income tax or any other tax. This is essentially the job of the Congress. A president may propose a tax program, but it must first be reviewed by the House of Representatives, more specifically the House Ways and Means Committee, and thereafter sent to the full House of Representatives for their approval and then on to the Senate for their approval, rejection, or modification. Once the congressional side is complete, the new tax bill or program is sent to the president for his signature (or rejection by way of veto). This is a brief summary of the process in place on how taxes are imposed on all U.S. taxpayers.

The president, here in the United States, for all intents and purposes is a figurehead with primarily a leadership role. What this means in simple language is that the president is largely responsible for guiding the nation through the various roads of governing in the areas of :

1--foreign policy and how we deal with other countries throughout the world

2-Proposing all types of programs that are designed to benefit U.S. citizens as a whole

3- National security

4- Taxes

5-Revsion of existing laws

6-Proposing new laws and budgets containing the broad outline of where revenues collected by the U.S. Treasury (from the many sources of taxation, royalties and fees and so on)will be spent each year.

The above process would cover just about all aspects of governing, up to and including natural disaster assistance due to hurricanes, earthquakes, volcanic eruptions, and tornadoes fiscal programs to stimulate or assist the national economy and so on. However, all the proposals made by any president must be approved by the legislative branch of government, commonly referred to as Congress. Members of Congress can also propose bills and programs for consideration that are reviewed and discussed. Eventually and through the combined actions of both the executive branch (the president) and the Congress, we end up with legislation being passed that enables our country to function year after year. The president does indeed have veto powers that allow him to reject spending bills proposed by Congress, but this is rarely used, since many objections are worked out before the bill is presented to the president for signature.

Moving on to more important matters that impact our disposable income, did you know that there are only two net revenue-generating agencies in the entire U.S. government? (They take in more revenue than the costs incurred in running the particular agency or department.)

The two agencies are the Internal Revenue Service and the U.S. Department of the Interior.

All other agencies of the U.S. government are engaged in net spending of some type, whether it is providing services to the nation such as the military in the area of our national security, the tax collectors at the IRS, or purchasing goods of all types necessary to deliver the federal services provided.

Before moving on to the main course of this chapter (U.S. federal income taxes), we need to spend a little time on the U.S. Department of the Interior (DOI), since it is an important source of both federal and state revenues without which our individual tax burdens would be far greater than they are today.

What is the US Department of the Interior? It is a Cabinet-level department of the U.S. government that principally manages federally owned land and other domestic type concerns. The operating units of the DOI include:

- National Park Service

- U.S. Fish and Wildlife Service

- Bureau of Indian Affairs

- Bureau of Land Management

- Minerals Management Service

- Office of Surface Mining

- U.S. Geological Survey

- Bureau of Reclamation

- Office of Insular Affairs

- Federal Executive Boards

The primary mission of the DOI, as it appears on their Web site at *www.interiordepartment.com,* is to:

- Protect the nation's natural, cultural, and heritage resources

- Manage domestic resources to promote responsible care and use in sustaining a dynamic economy

- Provide for domestic recreation through the care, conservation, and use of national parks, and ensure the protection of fish and wildlife

The DOI manages more than 500 million acres of surface land, or 20 percent of all land in the United States. The DOI is also responsible for a variety of water and underwater resources.

The Minerals Management Service or MMS collects billions of dollars each year on behalf of all U.S. citizens in the form of government royalties that result from the production of crude oil, natural gas, coal, and other natural resources.

Why is this so important for us to have a basic understanding of the DOI role in our lives? Most of the DOI activities, **including the billions of dollars in revenues they collect each year on our behalf in the form of royalties primarily from natural resource production,** translate their way into the cost we ultimately pay for all natural resource-based products we consume in the form of end-user products. This would include items such as gasoline we purchase at the pump for our cars and trucks, heating oil and natural gas for our homes, cosmetics, jet fuel for travel, coal to produce 50 percent of our electricity supply, to name just a few of the many items. In fact, more than 90 percent of everything produced requires some form of energy-related product input before final completion and consumption.

My point here is simple: if the federal government had more sources of revenue through a larger and expanding tax base, our ultimate individual income tax bills would be lower, **end of story.**

How do we develop more sources of revenue other than through various forms of taxation? **Economic growth through business expansion.** This is what was behind our dramatic growth into a global economic superpower over the past 100 years or so.

One present major potential revenue source would be created by allowing oil and natural gas companies in the United States to drill in U.S. coastal waters and the ANWR, both areas that are now off limits to any type of exploration and production. The recent high oil and gas prices brought just about everyone to the peak of financial stress and frustration. Congress again used the high energy cost crisis to play their games, with many senators and congressmen making all types of misleading statements about who is to blame and wanting to punish oil producers in the U.S. that are gouging the public by imposing a "windfall profits tax." However, very few of our elected officials called for expanding our own domestic energy supplies. This congressional behavior is nothing short of criminal, for multiple reasons set forth below.

- The entire United States economic engine requires energy resources to keep running. Our national security is also very dependent on energy supplies.

- Oil is a global commodity with base prices set by the Organization of the Petroleum Exporting Countries, commonly known as "OPEC." The United States (and all the U.S. oil companies as a group) is not a member of OPEC and therefore has virtually no hand in setting the oil price; global production demand automatically sets the price. This means that Americans must pay the internationally set OPEC price to get their share of oil they don't produce from American resources and desperately need. As this is the case, all the negative comments leveled at the United States oil-producing companies by our elected officials to make us believe they will do something to provide us with oil price relief or greater energy independence is nothing but hot air. The current reality is that rapidly developing countries such as China and India are creating unprecedented demand for oil and there simply is not enough excess production to go around.

- U.S. oil production has been declining for decades, causing oil imports to rise, with 60 percent of our current daily crude oil requirements being imported. The only two ways to reduce oil prices are to increase supplies (domestic supplies, for example from areas such as the U.S. coastal waters or the ANWR) or reduce demand. In less than three months, and as of November 15, 2008, reduced global oil demand has seen the global price of oil drop from over $145 down to approximately $36 per barrel on February 13, 2009.

The United States has substantial undeveloped oil and gas reserves that are off limits to production, compliments of our politically correct elected officials who worry just about everything except our domestic energy needs.

The ANWR area identified by the U.S. Geological Survey alone contains an estimated 11 billion barrels of oil and has the potential of being one of the largest-producing oil fields in North America. Yet Congress keeps blocking efforts to develop these resources, and we must all step back and ask why, when jobs, high energy costs, and less reliance on OPEC sources for our energy needs are at stake.

Another area containing vast supplies of oil and natural gas is our own U.S. coastal waters, where some 2 billion acres hold an estimated 80-plus billion barrels of oil and more than 400 trillion cubic feet of natural gas (equivalent to an additional 65-plus billion barrels of oil, converted by using a ratio of 6,000 cubic feet of gas having the same energy content as 1 barrel of oil). These potential quantities of oil and gas do not include shale resources oil.

While American companies are prohibited from drilling in U.S. coastal waters, all other countries around the world are drilling up every potential area and cannot get at their own reserves fast enough. China is now drilling in Cuban coastal waters less than sixty miles from Florida. Please keep in mind that oil-spill accidents that cause pollution to our waters have no boundaries, while environmental considerations that preclude us by regulation from drilling in most of our own coastal waters, we cannot stop others from drilling near our shores.

American oil companies have been drilling offshore in the Gulf of Mexico since the late 1950s. As of today, there has not been one major oil spill or other pollution-type accident in the Gulf since great care was taken in setting up the federal regulations necessary to ensure the potential for oil spills was minimized. Additionally, compliance with the safety regulations for offshore drilling was strictly adhered to by the American Oil Companies that produced over time the safest and best methods of drilling on the planet. Our technological know-how in this area of safety, pollution control, and accident-related minimization is now exported all over the world.

So what does all this have to do with us and our taxes? Well, using the data recited above, I will provide an example of how this impacts all U.S. taxpaying citizens.

Assume that the estimated untapped oil reserves mentioned above and totaling 156 billion barrels of oil equivalent (ANWR 11 billion, U.S. offshore 80 billion in oil and 65 billion in natural gas oil-equivalent barrels) of oil were targeted for development. As we all know, the federal government does not drill on federal acreage, but rather leases the acreage through the DOI to the major domestic oil companies for them to develop. This leasing process is conducted by bid price per acre, and a lease is awarded to the highest bidder, provided the price exceeds the minimum amount established by the DOI. Lease sales have brought in millions of additional dollars in revenue to the DOI, with little or no costs being incurred. Remember, the lease just gives the company a right to drill on the acreage for up to five years. If the exploration drilling results in no oil or gas being found, the lease usually expires at the end of the five-year period. On the other hand, if oil or gas is discovered, then the lease is said to be held by production (HBP) and will remain with the oil company for the entire productive life of the lease. Developing a lease to the point of production with pipelines in place to transport the production can take from two to five years or more, depending upon the logistical challenges that need to be addressed. Once production commences, the DOI, through the Minerals Management Service Department, collects a royalty on behalf of all the citizens of the United States. The royalty percentage is usually not less than one-sixth or 16.666 percent right off the top, before any costs incurred in getting the production out of the ground are deducted. So, for every $100 of oil or natural gas value produced, Uncle Sam collects $16.667. Applying simple math to the 156 billion barrels that can potentially be produced from the untapped resources, here is what we learn.

Let's assume that the price per barrel of oil is constant at fifty dollars over a production life of twenty years.

156 billion barrels divided by 20 years = 7.8 billion barrels of oil produced each year.

7.8 billion barrels of oil at $50 per barrel = $390 billion per year of new or incremental gross revenue. Moreover, this is $390 billion of U.S. money that is not being sent to the Middle East or other Organization of the Petroleum Exporting Countries ("OPEC") for the purchase of oil that we would now be producing from domestic U.S. sources.

$390 billion at the royalty rate of 16.667 percent to the federal government = $65 billion per year in new royalty revenues, representing all fresh new cash over and above the existing royalties currently being collected.

This is $65 billion that we will not have to come up with as taxpayers to fund federal expenditures (including the pork-barrel spending) and this is only the beginning of the food chain.

This oil and natural gas development activity will also create thousands of new jobs for many years when the companies spend the remaining $325 billion each year ($390 billion less the $65 billion in U.S. government royalties equals $325 billion in spending on equipment, materials, supplies, labor, transport of production, and so on). New jobs will create new taxpayers. Every dollar of payroll contributes 7.65 percent to Social Security and Medicare expenses that otherwise would have to come from somewhere else; this usually means the taxpayers and all the new employees will also be paying federal, state, and local income taxes on their earnings. The net take-home pay of the new employees who help develop our own domestic oil and gas resources is then spent on food, housing, cars, clothing, and other living expenses. This keeps our economy on the move and growing at the same time. The 7.8 billion barrels of oil and gas produced each year is then converted into a variety of products that heat our homes, provide energy to United States industries producing steel, cars, and thousands of other products, all of which generate many billions of dollars in revenues for multiple parties and new sources of incremental tax (sales, gasoline excise, and other taxes) for federal, state, and local governments. Again, this is less money that they will ask Joe the Taxpayer to cough up in some way, shape, or form; this only covers potential production from the ANWR and U.S. coastal waters that more than 60 percent of the people favored according to a Gallup Poll conducted in May 2008.

Shale oil and other domestic energy resources would contribute more money into the pot, sparing us the burden of more and more federal and state taxes we would otherwise have to pay. Engineers are presently working on refining shale rock primarily located in the Western United States into diesel or gas. If perfected, this will provide 2 trillion barrels of oil equivalents from the American West alone; this will provide enough energy to meet current U.S. demand for more than two centuries.

In my mind, all of the above is really something for all taxpayers in the United States to think about.

Oil and energy in general is very big business for the U.S. government (and all governments, for that matter, around the globe in countries that produce crude oil and natural gas). While many liberal-leaning politicians point fingers at big oil companies and their profits, the federal government's bottom-line profit from energy-related activities is more three times that of the oil companies. This is due to the royalty revenue collections coming right off the top of every dollar before any production or other expenses incurred to bring the product to the end consumer are deducted. In addition, most (if not all) oil- and natural gas-producing states impose production, severance, or ad valorem taxes on the value of production coming out of the ground (and this is in addition to the federal-level royalties and taxes).

Our elected political representatives are fully aware of the billions in government revenues generated by the oil industry and that the same revenues are a primary source of the very money they spend so freely.

Hopefully all readers now better understand the role of the Department of the Interior and its potential impact on our final individual income tax bills.

ON TO TAXES

The majority of U.S. citizens find the current system of taxation very complex and confusing. This is not by accident, for sure. The root cause for all the perceived complexity is the dissemination of conflicting information about taxes by too many different sources that only provide pieces of the facts (truth) about taxes. When the fact-based truth is published periodically by reputable resources such as the Tax Foundation, IRS, or Congressional Budget Office, many newspapers fail to carry the full story with all the details. Moreover, many people see an article on taxes and simply get turned off. A majority of them don't bother reading it and mistakenly prefer instead to rely on a politician to explain it to them during the campaign season; this is where the first big mistake is made by Joe the Taxpayer. For this reason, I thought that a book focusing on the significant tax-related areas that impact most people using simple illustrations and explanations for each area presented would be very helpful in understanding what is really going on in this black box we all know as taxation here in the United States.

Let's first start with a more meaningful understanding of income taxes on our earnings and investments. Investments will cover interest and dividend income, capital gains, rental, royalty, and other income from a variety of possible resources.

In the government fiscal year 2007 (ending September 30, 2007), the Tax Foundation at *www.taxfoundation.com* reported that ***Americans paid a record $2.568 trillion in taxes to the IRS,*** an increase of 6.7 percent over 2006. If you can believe it, the record tax collections reduced the federal budget deficit by 35 percent over fiscal year 2006, down to a level of $161 billion— and this is after all the expense outlays for the wars in Iraq and

Afghanistan plus all the new incremental expenses of homeland security since the 9/11 Islamic terrorist attacks on our country. We don't hear or read about these facts much, and therefore, the majority of Americans are totally unaware of what is going on in the tax arena as to how much tax revenue is collected and why taxes are up over the prior years.

The bulk of the income-tax collections are the result of basic income taxes on wages earned, corporate income taxes on profits (yes, Exxon Mobil may have earned $10 to 20 billion in profits that year, but this is after paying federal and state income taxes of $4 to 9 billion), and capital gains realized by taxpayers. Can you imagine what our individual tax bill would be here in the United States if Exxon Mobil did not pay such taxes? Do you think the politicians would cut spending or simply raise taxes to make up for the missing revenues from Exxon Mobil that they love to spend on special-interest pork-barrel spending that they refuse to make illegal?

Salaries and Wages Income

Income tax on salaries and wages is very simple to understand, since withholdings are estimated each payday using standard withholding tables or flat rates provided by the IRS applied to the gross income of each individual.

All compensation earned by individuals from personal services provided (no matter what form of payment cash or other non-cash consideration) must be included in tax reportable compensation for the year in which is was received by the taxpayer. Compensation will include salaries, commissions, bonus payments, taxable fringe benefits, consulting and other fees of any kind, profits payments, unemployment payments, retirement and pension payments, and any other form of compensation not mentioned. If the personal services compensation is not paid in cash but rather in property, the fair market value of the property at the time of receipt must be included in the taxpayers gross income.

At the end of each calendar year, all workers legally employed in the United States are provided with a form W-2 from their employer that summarizes; 1) all income earned for the calendar year just ended; 2) all tax withholdings made by employers on behalf of federal, state, and local income-tax authorities; 3) social security and Medicare tax withholdings; and 4) any other deductions from our gross pay, including 401(k) savings account contributions. This W-2 income information is necessary for each of us to prepare our annual income tax returns that will also include deductions permitted under existing IRS or local tax regulations, thus reducing our actual income tax bill for the year. Although this explanation appears simple enough, one cannot immediately conclude that when you earn more income in a given year, your tax bill likely goes up; this is very true, but not in many cases. **On the other hand, we cannot also conclude that if tax rates are raised by the government, income-tax collections will go up, since quite the opposite effect may result with collections actually falling, as we will see a little later on.**

Interest Income

All interest payments that we receive are fully taxable, with the exception of the following types of interest income:

- Tax-exempt municipal bonds issued by a state or local government authority.

- A limited amount of employee stock ownership plan loans.

- Interest from U.S. savings bonds that is used to pay for certain educational expenses.

Certain interest items that are accrued (although not actually received in hand by the taxpayer) are also taxable. This would include interest that is credited periodically and related to certificates of deposit (CD) that can be withdrawn **without paying** a penalty before the CD matures. If there is a penalty for such an interest withdrawal, the interest is not taxable until the CD matures.

Dividend Income

Dividends represent payments by a corporation out of its earnings and profits to the shareholders/owners of the corporation. The dividend can be either "ordinary" or "qualified" and received in cash and/or property; Dividends are generally taxed as ordinary income. If the dividend is paid in cash, the amount of cash received is the amount reported as ordinary dividend income. If the dividend is in property or part cash and part property, the fair market value of the property plus the cash component must be reported as ordinary dividend income in the year received.

Qualified dividends paid to shareholders of a corporation between January 1, 2003 and December 31, 2010 are taxed at lower tax rates than ordinary income, compliments of the Bush administration tax cuts. To claim a qualified dividend on a particular stock, investors are required to own the stock for more than sixty days.

Stock dividends (as opposed to the usual cash dividends paid) received by a taxpayer and the value thereof are generally not includible in gross income by the stockholder/taxpayer until the stock received is sold; at that point, it then becomes a realized tax event.

Rent and Royalty Income

Rental income generally results from ownership of property by a taxpayer, who in turn leases out the property to another person or entity in return for a periodic payment known as rent. The owner of the property is referred to as the "lessor" and the party who rents the property is referred to as the "lessee."

All rental income received by a lessor must be included in gross income. If the lessee pays for expenses of the lessor, this too would represent additional rental income to be reported. All expenses incurred by the lessor in producing the income from the property are deductible in arriving at adjusted gross income.

Royalty income can be realized from many sources, including patents on inventions, production of oil, gas, or other mineral properties, copyrights on artistic works such as musical, literary, and other similar property.

Capital Gains and Losses

The sale or exchange of capital-type assets by taxpayers (individuals or corporations) can result in what is known as a capital gain or loss that would be reported on the tax return filing for the calendar or fiscal year in which the transaction closed. A capital asset is any property including stocks, bonds, homes, real estate, and the like, but does not include certain items such as:

- Inventory or other property held for resale to customers in the ordinary course of a taxpayer's trade or business

- Real property used in a trade or business

- Business property that is depreciable

The capital gain or loss realized by a taxpayer can either be short- or long-term in nature. A capital asset must currently be held for more than twelve months to be considered a long-term capital gain or loss. If an asset is sold or exchanged after being held for less than a twelve-month period, the resulting gain or loss is characterized as a "short-term capital gain or loss." The significance of long- versus short-term is the associated tax liability or benefit that goes along with the transaction. Short-term gains are taxed at ordinary higher income rates while long-term gains are taxed at a lower, more attractive rate. This lower tax rate encourages investment in a variety of activities that is vital to our economic growth and well-being.

Capital gains or losses are determined by netting the cost of the capital asset against the proceeds received from the sale. To illustrate, if you purchased a stock for $100 per share and then sold it for $150 net of selling expenses, you would realize a capital gain on the transaction of $50. If the holding period for this stock was only eleven months, the gain would be short term and the tax would be calculated by applying ordinary rates at, say, 30 percent to the $50 gain and taxes to be paid would total $15 (.30 x $50 = $15). On the other hand, if the holding period for this stock was fourteen months, the tax due would be calculated using the long-term rate of 15 percent, and the tax due would be only $7.50, a 50 percent decrease (.15 x $50 = $7.50). Clearly one can see the significant tax benefit applied to long-term gains, hence the reason the capital gain tax rate is always a hot topic button, as we will see a little later on.

Losses that result from capital transactions in a given tax year are first offset against any gains. Short-term losses would first be offset against short-term gains, and long-term losses would be offset against long-term gains. For individuals, if after the netting process short-term losses still remain, they are deducted from gross income, but this deduction is limited to only $3,000 per year for a jointly filed income tax return ($1,500 for a single individual). Corporate taxpayers can only deduct losses to the extent of any gains reported. The losses that cannot be utilized in a given tax year can be carried forward and deducted from tax returns filed in the future for an unlimited number of years.

The Bush administration tax-cut proposals that were passed by the U.S. Senate and House of Representatives in

2003 included a reduction of the capital gains tax rate down to 15 percent from 20 percent. Although this tax rate went down by 25 percent, U.S. Treasury tax collections from capital gains transactions rose by more than 150 percent in the four-year period following the 2003 cut (as reported at *www.irs. gov*) . In calendar year 2002, tax filers reported $269 billion in capital gains, and in calendar year 2007, filers reported capital gains of more than $850 billion. A good amount of the gains were indeed tied into rising stock and real estate prices, but the lower capital gains rates induced investors to cash in their gains and take the profits, as the associated tax liability was not that great. This condition of low tax rates allows investors to realize the gains sooner and re-invest the net proceeds. Yes indeed, Uncle Sam only gets 15 percent of tax on the gain and not the 20 percent, but there are so many more transactions to collect taxes on because investors care less about the taxes when the rate is lower.

The capital gains tax cut in 2002 was a big win for Uncle Sam, since tax collections from capital gains transactions shot up over $125 billion in 2007 from $49 billion in 2002. The higher capital gains revenue helped reduce the budget deficit and also partly eliminated the need for tax-rate increases on other income, including salaries and wages earned by all taxpayers.

Given all the new Federal revenue unlocked by the cut in capital gains tax rates, why during the recent presidential campaign did Barack Obama and Hillary Clinton advocate an increase in the capital gains rate up to 28 percent and 20 percent, respectively? Didn't they realize that an increase would very likely reduce Uncle Sam's annual revenues substantially? They claimed that the low rates benefit the "rich" investor community. This is not the case at all, since all investors benefit from the lower rate; there are more than 115 million investors in the United States, or more than one-third of the entire population. In fact, the Congressional Budget Office *(www. cbo.gov)* reported that for the calendar year 2005, 79 percent of tax returns filed reporting capital gains were from filers with incomes of less than $100,000 for the year.

Reported dividend income has also increased by 50 percent since the tax rate on dividends was cut down to 15 percent from 40 percent in 2003. This would mean that a good deal of the income gains reported by the federal government in the last few years is the result of taxpayers converting their assets into taxable income just so that they can take advantage of the lower capital gains tax rate.

Given the factual data reported by numerous groups—such as the Congressional Budget Office *(www.cbo.gov)*, The Tax Foundation *(www.taxfoundation.com)*, and the IRS *(www.irs.*

gov)— over the past five years that the lower capital gains tax rates have provided a windfall of extra tax revenue to the federal treasury, why would anyone increase taxes simply to get more money out of the so-called "rich"? The reality is that, in reviewing the capital gains area and historical data recited above that deals with the rate and revenues collected by the government, the higher rates would negatively affect more than 115 million U.S. investors. The smart move would be to lower the rates some more, or at the very least keep them where they were in 2008. Perhaps the recent financial crisis that has sent shockwaves through the entire U.S. and global economies will give everyone a second chance to reconsider whether any tax increases in the foreseeable future are really a wise move. The facts on capital gains rates and the related impact on U.S. Treasury revenue collections are very clear and well documented. **When the capital gains tax rate rises (as demonstrated over the past fifty years or so), reported capital gains decline dramatically and federal revenue collections naturally decline as well. Lower federal revenue collections means less money available for many of the social programs helping the genuinely poor and needy U.S. citizens (and illegal immigrants as well). This is why we cannot believe most of what the liberal senators and congressman say about only the rich benefitting from lower capital gains rates. It is simply not true and is very misleading to all investor/taxpayers.**

A good question to ask at this point is who makes up the more than 115 million investors in the United States? Well, just about every working or retired citizen in the country with a retirement pension or other savings strategy of some kind, whether it is contributory or non-contributory. This includes all public and private **union pension trust funds,** individual retirement accounts (IRAs), 401(k) retirement savings plans (401(k) savings), total deferred annuities (TDA), and the like. All such plans holding investor savings and contributed funds are invested in stocks, bonds, mutual funds, index funds, and so on by financial experts and other professionals who manage the assets. Regrettably, the estimated market losses incurred by such savings and retirement funds since the beginning of 2008 here in the United States alone are in the trillions of dollars for the reasons mentioned elsewhere in this book.

Federal Income Tax Facts

Income tax statistics are regularly gathered but usually reported to the public two or three years after the data has been assembled and analyzed by the various government agencies. For example, in late December 2007, the Congressional Budget Office and IRS released tax statistics for calendar year 2005 that revealed the not-so-surprising facts listed below.

- The richest 1 percent of all taxpayers earned 21 percent of all the income reported and paid 39 percent of all the taxes collected by the IRS for that tax year.

- The richest 5 percent of all taxpayers (including the 1 percent group above) earned 36 percent of all the income reported and paid 60 percent of all the taxes collected by the IRS for that tax year.

- The richest 10 percent of all taxpayers (including the two groups above) paid 70 percent of all the taxes collected by the IRS for that tax year.

- These tax amounts reported are all up sharply since 1990, when the richest 1 percent of all taxpayers earned 14 percent of all the income reported and paid 25 percent of all the taxes collected by the IRS for 1990, compared to 39 percent in 2005. In that same year (1990), the richest 5 percent earned approximately 27 percent of all the income reported and paid only 44 percent of all the taxes, collected compared to 60 percent in 2005.

- Half of all the households (more than 50 million of them) paid only **3 percent** of all income taxes collected in 2005.

Taxing the rich at higher tax rates to supposedly provide relief to the poor and middle class never works in practice, but reducing tax rates does in fact work. To illustrate, in 1981, the highest income tax rate was 70 percent and the top capital gains rate was 45 percent. The richest 1 percent of Americans at that time paid only 17 percent of the total income taxes collected, compared to 39 percent collected in 2005, when the top income tax rate was only 35 percent and the capital gains rate was only 15 percent. The change from 1981 to 2005 resulted in a whopping increase of 129 percent in tax collections from the top 1 percent of richest taxpayers. Why? The lower tax rates serve as an incentive for people to cash in on gains sooner so that they can move on to other investment opportunities, plain and simple. If these unquestionable facts reported by the IRS do not amaze and impress each reader in light of all the misinformation communicated to us by many of our own politicians, nothing will—and your basic understanding of income taxes is hopelessly doomed.

During this same period (1981 to 2005), 75 to 80 percent of the taxpayers making up the middle- and lower-income groups paid only 14 percent of all income taxes paid in 2005; in 1981, this same group paid 28 percent of all the taxes paid or a full 50 percent drop in their tax burden. This tells us that the only group that really experienced significant increases in their taxes was the top 5 percent of the taxpayers. Again, the facts show that when you cut the highest tax rates on the highest income earners, the government collects more money from them. When you cut taxes for the other 95 percent of the taxpayers (Mr. Obama's campaign promised that 95 percent of the taxpayers would get a tax cut during his tenure as president), the government collects less money.

Many governments around the world are quickly lowering their tax rates, since they have discovered (not surprisingly) that lower rates bring in more revenues and attract both domestic and foreign investors to expand and grow the tax base. Despite this reality, the U.S. Congress is still pushing to raise the highest income tax rate from 35 percent to 39.3 percent without extending the Bush administration tax cuts. If this in fact happens, the highest income tax rate actually will rise to 44 percent.

What Is the Next Best Course of Action for U.S. Tax Rates?

Well, the global financial collapse in late 2008 that started in the United States was caused by a multitude of bad public and private policies, a breakdown in banking and investment community regulatory oversight, and errors in judgment by many, including politicians, bankers, insurers, and other executives tied to the financial community—to name a few of the guilty. The financial carnage will no doubt bring about some very necessary changes in both industry and all levels of government, starting with the elimination of all unnecessary spending (highly unlikely) and a likely postponement of any federal tax increases promised by the new incoming president in an attempt to revive the U.S. economy.

As mentioned earlier in chapter 2, the Alternative Minimum Tax (or AMT) was originally intended to ensure that a small number of wealthy taxpayers actually paid some taxes. This wealthy group of taxpayers managed to avoid paying any income taxes by reporting very substantial deductions from their gross income despite significant levels of reported income. For many years, this AMT affected less than 1 percent of all taxpayers, but this has changed in recent years. In fact, in 2005, the AMT impacted almost 3 percent of all taxpayers, and if left unchanged, it is expected to impact 20 percent of the taxpayers by 2010; some 30 million filers earning between $50,000 and $200,000 will be the hardest hit. The primary cause for this expansion of the AMT and related exposure to many more taxpayers is that the AMT thresholds were never indexed for inflation, whereas regular income tax rates are. As we all know, with two income earners in many households, it is not difficult to find your household in this annual gross income earning range. A teacher or nurse married to a fireman or policeman, or any couple working in the public sector for either a large city or state, filing their tax return jointly can easily earn well over

$100,000 per year in many parts of the country, including the affluent suburbs and thus automatically become subject to the AMT.

So once more, I must state, to be perfectly clear and to dispel rumors and misleading statements made by many politicians that: The AMT only goes after the rich and their tax-sheltered investments. *The AMT erases most of the routine itemized deductions that lower the annual federal income tax bill for a substantial number of the middle-class households.*

How does this AMT work? The AMT has a standard deduction that protects a large number of taxpayer households. Here I must again remind every reader that 55 percent of all taxpayer households currently earn less than $50,000 of gross income and therefore totally escape the AMT.

The AMT has two tax brackets:

- 26 percent for gross incomes between $50,000 and $175,000.

- 28 percent for all those earning more than $175,000.

Once a taxpayer exceeds the income threshold of $50,000, many deductions that are allowed by the regular income tax regulations (including deductions for state and local income taxes paid, medical expenses, unreimbursed business expenses, and the like) start to disappear. In a nutshell, if you are a taxpayer with lots of itemized deductions (including the aforementioned items plus mortgage interest, real estate taxes on your home, contributions, and other so-called tax preferences including some passive investment activities), you will without doubt get caught in the AMT web. In fact, according to reports appearing on the Tax Foundation Web site *(www.taxfoundation.com)*, the U.S. Treasury estimates that the AMT alone will generate some $88 billion in tax revenue collections for the calendar year 2008, and this amount is expected to double in 2012. If the AMT is adjusted to provide relief to taxpayers caught in its web, how will our elected officials make up for any slowdown in this revenue stream? You can safely wager that it will be some other form of tax with a different name, shape, or form, to be sure.

Fortunately, in 2008, legislation was proposed and passed to provide some temporary relief from the AMT by extending for one year some tax exemptions and increasing the AMT exemptions from $33,750 to $46,200 for individual tax filers and from $45,000 to $69,950 for joint tax filers. Presumably, the exemption increase is designed to factor in adjustments for inflation that were not indexed in the original AMT formula. There are some other minor features in the relief legislation, but the biggest problem is that it is not permanent and will need to be addressed again, probably in 2009.

To illustrate how the AMT impacted a family in 2007 by increasing the tax bill, please see below. (All amounts are illustrative estimates only.)

Adjusted gross income for the year: $160,000

Reduced by Itemized deductions on federal return:

- State and local income taxes paid $6,613
- Mortgage Interest $19,200
- Property taxes paid $8,000
- All other itemized deductions $5,300
- Federal exemptions for family of 4 $20,300
  Total deductions $59,413

Regular Taxable Income   **$100,587**

Regular Tax before AMT $17,835

AMT Income is: $160,000

Less AMT exemption: $45,000 (a)

AMT Income is thus: $115,000

AMT tax on $115,000 $ 21,437

Resulting Additional AMT tax due: $3,602

(a) This exemption amount is phased out for joint tax filers as their AMT income goes up and totally eliminated when AMT Income reaches a level of $330,000. This would mean that if adjusted gross income for a successful professional couple filing jointly was $331,000, there would be no itemized deductions allowed in calculating the AMT tax due.

All amounts in the example above are purely illustrative, but provide the necessary picture on how much additional tax is brought about by the AMT. In this instance, the taxpayer was only allowed $45,000 of itemized deductions (the AMT exemption amount) even though his actual itemized deductions for the year were $59,413. **This is why the AMT is referred to as the "stealth tax," as many tax filers don't even know they are not getting the benefit for some of their deductions.** In this case, 24 percent of the itemized deductions are disallowed, and the result was a 20 percent increase in the final federal income tax bill from $17,835 to $21,437.

Taking a quick look back to 2001, we were in a moderate recession at that time, followed by the 9/11 terrorist attacks on American soil. The Bush administration's proposed income and investment tax cuts were approved by Congress; these changes were very necessary and successfully put life back into the U.S. economy by creating more than 7 million jobs in the years that followed the cuts through 2007 (as reported by the U.S.

Department of Commerce at *www.commerce.gov*). However, even though these federal-level tax cuts were real and benefited most if not all U.S. tax filers, state and local level property, school, and other taxes have been increasing dramatically, due largely to unchecked spending and out-of-control contract costs for many of the public sector unions and their workers in the area of salaries and benefits pre- and post-retirement. It is no surprise that many taxpayers like myself really don't see, believe, or realize the in-my-pocket benefit or effect of any tax cuts (everything taken together: federal, state, and local). It's also no surprise that this is all our elected officials seem to talk about on the campaign trail; I wonder if they ever get tired of trying to fool the people who have less and less to spend each year because of collective increased tax burdens.

Regrettably, the Bush administration income tax cuts are scheduled to expire in 2010 since our Congress did not make the cuts permanent. Consequently, many taxpayers (mostly concentrated in the over $100,000 gross income households) are looking at one of the largest and perhaps the worst tax hikes in our post-tax revolution history.

The U.S. (and global) economy is currently slowing down faster than at any time in our history; many significant and costly unfunded entitlements are coming due as the baby boomers start to retire (e.g., unfunded federal Social Security, drug, and Medicare benefits). Higher taxes that will slow the growth of our economy down are the last things we really need. Economic growth and a healthy tax revenue stream into the federal treasury is vital to our economic well-being as a nation, so let us hope our elected officials behave as statesmen in taking actions that grow and expand our economy, rather than following the historic pattern of attempting to redistribute income for political reasons by increasing unproductive spending. Unfortunately, the new 2009 stimulus package is loaded with unproductive spending programs, with very few new long-term jobs expected. Most of the funds will go to maintain education-related programs, welfare payments, and so on, with very little devoted to areas that will expand the economy and tax base. (Please see chapter 6 for additional details on this subject of the 2009 stimulus plan.)

There is really not much more to add on the very condensed subject of individual income taxes described in this chapter, but I sincerely hope that this attempt to provide a very brief but understandable overview of our complex U.S. individual income tax system is clear to all readers.

Corporate and Other Business Taxes

The federal income tax on corporations was first introduced in 1909 when corporate income above $5,000 in a given year was hit with a 1 percent tax.

Corporation and other business income taxes paid to the U.S. Treasury, combined with individual federal income taxes paid, are essential revenue streams necessary year after year to finance activities of the federal government for the benefit and well-being of all residents of the United States. In addition, many states also impose some type of income tax of their own on corporations.

If we did not impose income taxes on business activities, personal income taxes alone necessary to finance all government-(federal, state, and local) related activities would rise to levels that would make it impossible for many people to provide basic necessities for themselves just by earning a salary.

The bottom line here on the corporate and business income tax side of things in the United States (and elsewhere around the globe) is that increasing profits earned by corporations and other businesses in the United States results in a lower tax burden at the individual income tax level.

There are three primary categories of business entities described below.

Corporations in the United States are legally formed by one or more persons (investor shareholders/owners) in a particular state to engage in some form of business activity for the purpose of earning a profit that would ultimately be realized and divided among the investors/shareholders. Corporations have state-mandated regulations and requirements to oversee their activities and business conduct that is monitored by regulatory agencies and taxing authorities. The tax treatment of corporations may vary depending on the type of entity that determines if tax due on profits is payable by the corporation or directly by its shareholders/owners. The majority of corporate entities in the United States are either C corporations or S corporations.

C corporations are subject to the biggest tax bill, and their earnings are effectively taxed twice—once on the income they earn as a corporation (a legal taxable entity), and a second time when the income is distributed to shareholders/owners as dividends. The dividends must be reported on the individual tax return of the shareholder owner and taxed at the individual income tax level. This is how the C corporation income is effectively taxed twice.

S corporations do not pay any income taxes at all, since all of the income and expenses of the entity are passed on directly to the shareholders/owners, who then report the income and expenses on their own individual income tax returns. This treatment for S corporations with items of income and expense flowing directly to the individual income tax returns of the shareholders/owners is the manner in which partnership returns are treated.

S corporations are required to file what is referred to as an information tax return each year so that the corporation's activities can be matched up to the individual tax returns of the shareholders/owners.

S corporations must be a small business entity as defined by the Internal Revenue Code regulations, and must meet other eligibility requirements (including a limit on the number of shareholders it can have) before they can classified as an S corporation.

The S corporation was conceived to make it easier for people to establish a business enterprise that had many of the protections available to a C corporation without many of the other IRS reporting- and compliance-related burdens.

Partnerships in the United States come in a variety of different forms that are generally entered into by two or more persons (or other permitted groups) to conduct some type of business activity for the purpose of earning a profit for the partners. The profit-sharing arrangements between the partners can vary depending upon the partnership agreement entered into, but in the absence of a formal partnership agreement, the profits are assumed to be shared equally by each partner. Income taxes that must be paid from earnings of the partnership are reported by the individual partners on their personal income tax returns and not by the partnership itself. The partnership, however, is required to file an information type tax return each year on behalf of the partnership.

Sole proprietorship is the final category of business entity (and the largest group of businesses in the United States) that is established by an individual engaged in a business practice to earn a profit. There are very few required formalities to set up a sole proprietorship business activity, and it is the simplest form of business to conduct. Income earned by such an entity is reported by the individual owner on his or her individual income tax return each year. Federal, state, and local income tax return filings require specific detailed information about the entity revenues earned and expenses incurred in operating the business during the year, for the purposes of determining the correct income tax liability due on such activities, if any. If the business earned no income after deducting all expenses or actually realized losses in a particular year, there would naturally be no income taxes to be paid.

Corporate and other business income taxes are in effect double taxes from several vantage points since the business entity is taxed on profit earned, and again, as individual income when it is distributed to the shareholder/owners as a dividend or simply passed on to the individual partners or sole proprietors.

I can tell you that while many can correctly argue that this is a double tax, it is somewhat invisible to us as individual taxpayers. Therefore, the present system should not only remain in place to keep our individual income tax bill in check, but government incentive programs should also be in place to encourage expansion and growth of every U.S. business entity. This will keep the U.S. businesses competitive in the global marketplace so more and more profits can be earned, thus ensuring that our individual personal income tax bills don't get out of control. So how can we make sure that it gets done?

Well, the current U.S. corporate income tax rate is in the range of 35 to 38 percent, depending upon the amount of income. Currently, if a corporation has a taxable income of more than \$18.3333 million, the applicable rate is a flat 35 percent. Individual state and local income taxes are also imposed on business entities in some form, and this is in addition to the 35 percent imposed at the federal level.

State and local corporate tax rates can add anywhere from less than 1 percent to as much as 12 percent to the federal 35 percent burden, depending on where the company is located.

In foreign countries without state and local taxing authorities, these additional taxes are referred to as indirect-type taxes that in many European countries include the Value Added Tax (VAT) that also raises considerable amounts of revenue for the respective governments.

In addition to the regular corporate income tax, the AMT may be imposed on any corporation having tax preference items.

Certain corporations are used by their shareholders/owners to avoid paying taxes. To limit this type of abuse, such corporations would be subject to an accumulated earnings or personal holding company tax. These two taxes essentially get at the profits kept in the business so that the shareholders/owners do not have to pay taxes when the profits earned by the corporation are not paid out to them in the form of dividends.

Corporate and other business entities exist in just about every country around the world. Every country naturally has its own tax laws and regulations that the business entities must comply with. However, each government is very much aware of the competitiveness factor that exists in the global business community; for this reason, it will attempt to make its respective tax regulations more investor friendly to attract and encourage certain types of business behavior and practices that will increase the tax revenues of that country.

To illustrate how this competitive factor in the tax arena would work, the basic (or statutory) federal corporate tax rate in the U.S. is currently in the 35 percent average range, as mentioned earlier. The current statutory average corporate rate in Japan is 40 percent; Belgium, 34 percent; United Kingdom,

28 percent; Canada, 30 percent; and so on. The lower tax rates on business earnings simply means there is more money for the shareholders/owners at the end of each year. Why not set up shop in a country where you put more of the earnings in your own pocket? In the global economic environment that we all currently live in, the competitiveness of U.S.-based business entities is extremely important, and this, in my opinion, starts with tax-driven decision-making.

The Tax Foundation *(www.taxfoundation.com)* reported that for the period from 1990 to 2007, the U.S. has gone from a below-average corporate tax nation to the second highest rate in the industrial world (Japan takes top honors among the three largest economies in the world: the United States, China, and Japan), while many other countries have cut their corporate tax rates to as low as 10 percent.

Many countries let their native companies pay taxes in the country where the income is earned, as generally required by local tax laws and tax treaties in effect. However, many of the countries also tax income or capital that is returned to the native headquarters country (a movement of cash referred to as *repatriated income*). This added tax burden generally prompts companies to keep significant amounts of cash in foreign lands. Many countries are now seeking changes to their tax laws so that cash inflows start returning home for re-investment. The returning cash acts as a stimulus to the local economy through expansion of businesses and the creation of new jobs.

Regrettably, while foreign governments are reducing corporate tax burdens and inviting foreign investment, our U.S. Congress and the recent tax laws they propose to create will effectively keep capital and foreign investment money out of the United States. This logic follows the U.S. legislative attempts to raise a variety of income taxes that clearly stunt economic growth.

What can be done to keep up with the global corporate competition? Reduce the U.S. statutory corporate tax rates, maintain allowable deductions and tax incentives for businesses, and don't tamper with related tax regulations covering other business practices that drive investment decisions so that the United States remains competitive with tax rates around the world. Japan, Germany, Italy, Canada, Belgium, the United Kingdom, and many other countries on the listing below clearly demonstrate they each have or plan to cut their corporate tax rates in a clear attempt to attract foreign capital that will help stimulate their own economies.

OECD Nations Continue Cutting Corporate Tax Rates While U.S. Stands Still

Statutory Rates, Federal Plus Provincial/State, 2007 and 2008

Rank	Country	Combined Corporate Income Tax Rate, 2008	Combined Corporate Income Tax Rate, 2007	Change from 2007 to 2008
1	Japan	39.54%	39.54%	0
2	United States	39.25%	39.26%	0
3	France	34.43%	34.43%	0
4	Belgium	33.99%	33.99%	0
5	Canada	33.5%	36.12%	-2.6%
6	Luxembourg	30.38%	30.38%	0
7	Germany	30.18%	38.9%	-8.7%
8	Australia	30%	30%	0
9	New Zealand	30%	33%	-3%
10	Spain	30%	32.5%	-2.5%
11	Mexico	28%	28%	0
12	Norway	28%	28%	0
13	Sweden	28%	28%	0
14	United Kingdom	28%	30%	-2%
15	Italy	27.5%	33%	-5.5%
16	Korea	27.5%	27.5%	0
17	Portugal	26.5%	26.5%	0
18	Finland	26%	26%	0
19	Netherlands	25.5%	25.5%	0
20	Austria	25%	25%	0
21	Denmark	25%	25%	0
22	Greece	25%	25%	0
23	Switzerland	21.17%	21.32%	-0.1%
24	Czech Republic	21%	24%	-3%
25	Hungary	20%	20%	0
26	Turkey	20%	20%	0
27	Poland	19%	19%	0
28	Slovak Republic	19%	19%	0
29	Iceland	15%	18%	-3%
30	Ireland	12.5%	12.5%	0
	OECD Average	26.6%	27.6%	-1%

Source: OECD Organization for Economic Co-Operation and Development

In September 2008, the accounting firm KPMG released its annual survey results of corporate tax rates for 2008, indicating that the United States continues to maintain one of the highest overall corporate tax rates in the world.

The report also states that the global average corporate rate declined almost a full point to 25.9 percent when compared to rate of 26.7 percent in 2007, with the 2008 European Union average at 23.2 percent, the Latin American average at 26.6 percent, and the Asia Pacific average rate down to 28.4 percent. The report further indicated that twenty-three countries lowered their corporate tax rates in 2008.

The House Ways and Means Committee, which is responsible for proposing tax-related changes, is now controlled by the Democrats. Current proposals clearly focus on reducing the overall corporate tax rate from the 35 percent level to the 30 percent range; this is certainly focusing in on the competitive factor with foreign countries. However, when you look at the details of some other proposals in the total package of corporate tax changes, quite a different bottom line tax bill shakes out. For example, changes to corporate deductions related to interest on loans and the value of inventory will result in substantially higher net taxes to be paid. The result is that many companies will have a bigger tax bill that will more than offset the rate reduction from 35 to 30 percent. This is simply another deceptive practice that allows politicians to say they reduced the tax rate for our corporate entities to be competitive in the global arena, but because of the changes also made to deductions disallowed, the net tax bill actually goes up.

...another accounting practice that allows polluters to say they reduced their emissions from some previous... both comparative ... in the global ... but beyond ... if the change also made in predictions also lower the true risk bill and any cost to ...

CHAPTER 5

WASTEFUL USE OF OUR TAX DOLLARS AND THE TAXPAYER COST OF ILLEGAL IMMIGRATION

In the last several months of 2008 and into the new year 2009, many of the government, business, and individual financial excesses (borrowing and spending) that we all have been availing ourselves of finally became fully visible to everyone with severe financial wreckage in its wake. This includes the collapse of the housing industry, multiple banks, and other financial institutions; rising unemployment; and investment losses in the trillions of dollars to more than 150 million Americans alone. This culminated in a near-total shutdown of virtually all credit markets on the planet with an overall crushing blow to the global economy.

At this time, many people in the United States and around the world are frightened and very concerned about the near-

and long-term consequences of the recent financial crisis. They have initially responded by substantially reducing all non-essential spending and increased their rate of savings.

Many corporate and other businesses have also responded to this meltdown by implementing a series of self-preservation measures designed to keep them afloat until the economic recovery begins. The measures include staff reductions, elimination of certain (if not all) discretionary expenditures, and an all-important category we refer to in a Company that I worked at as "bad costs." Bad costs are those expenses that have no identifiable benefit that can and should be avoided with no harm to the business. Good costs, on the other hand, include expenses that provide some immediate and ongoing future benefit to the business. This benefit is either in the form of personnel work efficiencies or the ability for the existing operations as a whole to expand without additional fixed costs being incurred.

As a nation, we are currently facing a giant black hole of expenditures brought about by the various government stimulus efforts necessary to avoid additional financial calamity. For this reason, we must insist that our representatives at the federal, state, and local levels of government not only reduce overall spending in terms of absolute dollars spent compared to the prior year, but that they also eliminate any bad costs as well.

Failure to do so will create very regrettable hardship conditions for just about every citizen in the United States.

In fact, and not surprisingly, in early 2009, many legislators in the large "big-spend" states are resisting job cuts, salary reductions, and social welfare program cuts that would clearly prove to be very unpopular to everyone but the bottom-line taxpayer. The local officials prefer to seek federal bailout money and also increase taxes on Joe the Taxpayer, who once again gets stuck with not only the local bill, but the tab for all the federal bailout money for the next two dozen years or so— while he struggles to stay in his own home and put food on his table.

Government bad costs would appropriately include expenditures related to illegal immigration, Medicare and Medicaid fraud or abuse, birthright citizenship, foreign aid, pork-barrel spending, and other non-essential projects or expenditures.

It is estimated that Medicare and Medicaid fraud and abuse (federal and state combined) has an annual taxpayer cost of more than 10 percent of total benefits paid out by the government. If you believe that the estimated 2008 Medicare and Medicaid net expenditures of $601 billion, an amount that will increase at the same 7 percent rate that 2007 comparable net expenditures increased (net cost was $562 billion in 2007 compared to $524 billion in 2006 as reported by the Centers for Medicare & Medicaid Services (CMS) 2007 CFO Annual Report *(www.cms.hs.gov))*, it would mean that approximately $60 billion of our taxpayer dollars could be chalked up to pure waste or what we can call bad costs. I cannot determine if the estimated 10 percent fraud and abuse rate includes the care cost of illegal immigrants or not. The 2007 CFO Annual Report provided very limited illegal immigrant statistics and projection assumptions going out to the year 2085, but the assumed number of illegal immigrants was not provided; the report more than likely did not include such costs to keep future cost projections low.

CMS is a federal agency within the Department of Health and Human Services (HHS) that administers Medicare, Medicaid, and other related health insurance programs in collaboration with all the states. CMS is the largest purchaser of health care in the world.

One of the key stated objectives in the CMS 2007 annual report is to reduce the percentage of improper payments (bad costs) made under the programs they administer. Improper payments cover paying the correct amount to legitimate providers for services provided to eligible beneficiaries; it does not include the raw fraud and abuse component, as the report on this aspect is unclear. However, the report did clearly state that fiscal year 2007 had an indicated gross paid claims error rate of 3.9 percent under the Medicare program alone, which amounted to $10.8 billion in gross improper payments. While this amount is enormous, the CMS agency met its goal for the year 2007 by reducing the error rate down to 4 percent or less against the 2004 base year, when the improper payments were just over 10 percent (again, not including outright fraud and abuse).

Despite this very respectable improvement in the area of improper payments since the year 2004, the independent auditors for CMS (Price Waterhouse Coopers) issued the customary annual report for 2007 that included a narrative report on internal controls in effect at CMS—and it was not good. More specifically, material weaknesses in the area of processing controls, including general, automated and systems application related controls. Additionally, significant deficiencies were noted in the financial reporting systems, processes, and lack of an integrated financial management system.

With more than 50 million recipients of Medicare and Medicaid benefits, one can only imagine how difficult it is to manage such a large government bureaucracy, not to mention the cost and effort required to minimize all types of improper payments, including abuse and fraud. Nevertheless, spending the required money to eliminate material weaknesses in the process and controls areas (good costs) would certainly provide substantial benefits to taxpayers who ultimately paid the bills. This is what we should all be demanding of our elected officials during every federal and state election campaign.

One other little-known or -discussed area of significant taxpayer cost in providing health care benefits involves the Emergency Medical Treatment & Labor Act (EMTALA) passed by Congress in 1986. EMTALA ensures public access to emergency services **regardless of ability to pay**. To summarize the requirements of this act, all Medicare-participating hospitals (this would include most hospitals except the very elite private hospitals) that have an emergency department must provide examination and treatment for a medical condition, including women in labor, whether or not they are eligible for benefits under the federal regulations governing the act. If the hospital determines that the individual has an emergency medical condition, the hospital *must* provide such treatment as may be required to stabilize the medical condition, and not release the patient until he or she has been stabilized. You ask, "What can the average taxpayer conclude from this language?"

Well, now you know how it is possible for any U.S. citizen or illegal immigrant without health coverage to walk into a Medicare-participating hospital and get treatment for his or her medical condition, including a woman about to give birth.

Needless to say, the cost of providing the services under EMTALA to millions of people can and does already cost U.S. taxpayers billions of dollars each year.

Now we must attempt to understand the urgency of health care reform that all our elected Democratic representatives in Congress talk about on the campaign trail and every other chance they get to ring this fire bell. Make no mistake about it: this "reform" we keep hearing about will certainly lead us down the path to socialized medical care in the United States. The political spin on this health care reform initiative that will be pumped up by our politicians is without limits. They will tell us that many babies and children are currently without coverage tearing at the heart of our human side and how this condition should be eliminated through health care reform. The objective of pushing reform is to have us believe that we will all be in medical care heaven (taxpayers, non-taxpayers, illegal immigrants all) once the health care reform program is in place and debugged. The democrats in control of congress will attempt to legislate this reform in 2009 promising billions in savings implementation taking several years, of course. In the end, we will have very few of the medical care choices we have today under the existing private setup (including Medicare and Medicaid) that provides most with some of the best medical services in the world. In many countries with socialized medical care programs in place, people needing non-life-threatening treatment must generally wait long periods of time for a multitude of medical services. My simple question is, "Why do we need to go down this path at all, when the current system is truly not broken, with several safety nets already in place created by law?"

We have heard over and over again by many political powers in the Democratic Party that there are some 45 million people in the United States without medical coverage. Let us assume that this estimate of the population without coverage is accurate for purposes of developing a list of logical questions that are never publicly addressed.

1. How many people do not have medical coverage in the United States because they have elected not to have it due to the high cost of such insurance, as was the case with two of my own adult professional children? It is has been reported in news articles many times over the past several years that millions of single young adults who are in the age range of eighteen to forty likely take a pass if they cannot afford this health care coverage expense. This decision is made with the belief that their young age and general health condition does not make this expense a priority. The monthly cost of single coverage can be in the range of $200 to $600 (depending on the menu of benefits provided) while family coverage can cost as much as $1,000 per month or more. Since this coverage cost comes out of disposable income, the person paying for family coverage would need to devote his first $18–20,000 of gross annual earnings to health care insurance alone if his employer did not have a program in place.

2. How many of the young adults described in question 1 above know that in the event of an medical emergency, they can go to a Medicare-participating hospital and by U.S. federal law, get the necessary medical treatment they need? You would be making a very safe bet to conclude that most of the illegal immigrants, including all the pregnant women here illegally, are fully up to date on all the legal details as to medical treatment that must be provided to them under existing U.S. law, complements of the U.S. taxpayers. This is the very reason many emergency rooms around the country are overwhelmed with mostly illegal immigrants, many of whom cannot speak a word of English, seeking care for a variety of medical conditions, many not life-threatening, up to and including the flu.

3. How possible is it that the approximately 45 million people in the United States without medical coverage includes more than 12 to 20 million illegal immigrants? My guess is that it does, but this question is never raised or made clear in the political spin. I have never heard a politician say that approximately 45 million U.S. citizens, including their children,

around the country are in need of health care for a **medical condition,** only that they are without **medical coverage.** Believe very little of what you hear from our political spin masters, and a little more of what you may read in print, keeping in mind the current financial mess they have steered us into with so many bad decisions over the years. **Here you must think for a moment about the Social Security Program problems and all the debt we have as a nation. This is mostly the result of wasteful and out-of-control past spending, fraud, mandated program abuses, catering to special interests and lobbyists (such as large companies, trial lawyers, and unions that contribute millions to election campaigns so that they can influence the passage of costly programs and other non-essential spending by elected officials), and finally, the illegal immigration mess and its cost),** all at the expense of Joe the Taxpayer.

4. Has anyone addressed or asked why the cost of health care is so high in this country? Does the cost of medical-related litigation estimated to be in the billions of dollars each year have anything to do with it? Are the large settlements in medical malpractice cases perhaps driving the out-of-control high cost of medical malpractice insurance that must be passed on to the people by the health insurance companies and doctors? Did anyone perhaps think that rather than coming up with a national health care program to ensure broad coverage for the citizens of the United States, that medical malpractice litigation reform might result in such substantial savings that the cost of medical insurance coverage might come down and thus become more affordable for the millions who elect not to have it due to high cost? These are the questions that should be asked of and answered by all our elected officials, and we must demand it at every opportunity.

5. Will U.S. taxpayers be asked to pay additional taxes for the cost of insuring the 45 million uninsured, many of whom either don't want the coverage or are illegal immigrants in the first place? The simple answer is *absolutely* yes, since Joe the Taxpayer ultimately must pay all the bills, no matter how many years or generations it may take.

I think just about everyone can agree that there are many people in the United States who simply cannot afford health care coverage and it really would be nice if they could have it. However, with the ability to obtain emergency medical treatment at most hospitals in the United States by law, how much of a priority should be made of it at additional taxpayer expense? **In closing this subject, one can safely assume that by law, no child, adult, pregnant woman, senior, or illegal immigrant will go without required medical treatment if they go to a hospital with an emergency room already funded by the taxpayer in some way.**

FEDERAL SPENDING OUT OF CONTROL:

The Office of Management and Budget *(www.omb.gov)* and Heritage Foundation *(www.heritage.org)* reported that federal expenditures by primary category increased substantially during the fiscal years 2001 through 2008 as shown below.

- Community Development 90 percent (or more than three times the combined annual inflation rate for the same period).

- National Defense 65 percent (or more than two times the combined annual inflation rate for the same period).

- Veterans Benefits 58 percent (or more than two times the combined annual inflation rate for the same period).

- Education 57 percent (or more than two times the combined annual inflation rate for the same period).

- Health Research 55 percent (or more than two times the combined annual inflation rate for the same period).

- Medicare 51 percent (or more than two times the combined annual inflation rate for the same period.

- Highway and Mass Transit 22 percent

- Social Security 17 percent

- Energy-related   16 percent

Keep in mind that inflation, during the same period that the expenditures listed above were increasing, was very much under control and below the annualized rate of 3.5 percent

Given the above facts, how can anyone argue that the "Bush tax cuts," as many Democrats claim, are at the heart of the budget problems in this country when the Congressional Budget Office stated, "substantial increases in spending are on an unsustainable path"? This is all before the current 2008/2009 financial crisis popped up out of the box and the real government spending in the trillions of dollars had to kick in to save the country.

Since the Democrats took control of Congress in 2006, federal expenditures are up over $425 billion. Some of the excessive spending areas included in the increase and reported by the Congressional Budget Office were:

- A record farm subsidy bill even though farm income was at record levels due to high commodity prices

- Community development

- Extended unemployment benefits

- Increases in veterans' benefits

- Aid for homeowners in deep trouble

Again, the expenditure increases are before aid to Detroit to keep the three primary car companies afloat, a proposed second stimulus bill, and most important of all before the 2008 stock market 'and financial system collapse that shut down credit markets putting the U.S. and global economies in a tailspin.

One would hope that our current national financial dilemma would convince our elected representatives at all levels of government to stop with the catering to special interests, pork-barrel spending, and earmarks that cost taxpayers billions of extra dollars each and every year, but that is simply asking for too much. And here is the reason why: On January 11, 2009, Yahoo news reported that "Congress is considering whether to set aside more that 2 million acres in nine states as wilderness in an early showdown that threatens to derail pledges by Senate leaders to work cooperatively as a new administration takes office." A similar bill last year was scrapped when Republican Senator Coburn from Oklahoma claimed the spending in the bill was too excessive with some $4 billion to be spent over five years and stated that the "earmark-laden" measure "makes a mockery of voters' hope for change." The spending would not only include wilderness protection, but also designate the childhood home of former President Clinton in Arkansas as a historic landmark, provide $3 million for a "road to nowhere" in

Alaska, provide $460 million to save 500 salmon in California, $3.5 million to celebrate the 450th birthday of St. Augustine, Florida, to name a few of the earmarks. The bill information can be found at *http://thomas.loc.gov* Bill S.22.

MOVING ON

Illegal immigration costs, a huge nightmare area for everyone in this country, represent a significant portion of the bad costs at the federal, state, and local levels of government. It also represents a very serious problem created by our federal government because of its failure to enforce existing laws over many years designed to prevent any illegal immigration into this country. It has cost taxpayers billions of dollars each year in the form or extra costs to many public school systems and hospitals, not only in the border states, but all around the country as these illegal immigrants spread out in search of employment. Schooling and medical costs are the most visible of the many additional costs related to illegal immigration that are funded almost exclusively by our tax dollars. It also drains state and local budgets in other ways, such as through the expense of incarcerating illegal immigrants who came into the United States and committed crimes in our communities. While more than 95 percent of the illegal immigrants may be law-abiding and not looking for trouble, the number of them who do commit crimes all over the country is staggering. The

California and Arizona prison systems are overwhelmed with more than a quarter of a million such residents.

How did all of this illegal immigration activity, mostly from Mexico, come about in the first place? Below is a brief list of what in my opinion were/are the primary drivers behind illegal immigration from Mexico.

- Limited economic growth and expansion in Mexico as a whole over the past thirty years or so (when compared to the United States).

- Lack of many educational and social programs in Mexico to address many of the problems of their large, unskilled labor force.

- Failure of the U.S. federal government legislators to deal effectively with illegal immigrants coming through our borders over many years.

- Failure of the U.S. federal government legislators to develop a fair and reasonable guest worker program that would have severely limited the number of illegal immigrants from remaining here in the United States, especially those employed as farm workers.

- The great American lie that everyone in the United States should and must go to college. Currently, a majority of native U.S. citizens very rarely consider careers as plumbers, electricians, carpenters, masons, roofers, factory workers, mechanics, laborers, farmers, technicians skilled in repairing a variety of hardware and other essential equipment we use daily either at work or home. The big question is why not? Education in the United States is now simply big business, and nobody seems to want their child to pursue careers in the trade areas because someone else can do that. Well, guess what? There are probably more than 12 million illegal immigrants holding such jobs here, because legal U.S. citizens are unwilling to pursue them.

A recent comprehensive study conducted by Robert Rector, a scholar at the Heritage Foundation, suggests that nearly two-thirds of the current estimated 20 million illegal immigrants fall into the category of low or unskilled labor, the group that his study was focused on. While the statistics for this category of worker may be accurate, over a limited period of time working in specific areas, these low or unskilled workers became the backbone of many trades areas relied on by small businesses throughout the entire country, especially in the area of housing and related construction.

Over the past twenty years, this growing problem of illegal immigration has been discussed openly on talk radio and certain TV shows, but not by our elected officials, who attempt to avoid the subject completely like a plague. As a result of this inaction over the years on the part of government at every level, the illegal immigration problem is out of control.

Birthright citizenship is also a major related issue of illegal immigration. The Center for Immigration Studies *(www.cis. org)* estimates that 380,000 children are born each year to illegal alien mothers, representing almost 10 percent of all births in the United States. Many of these women come here illegally for the sole purpose of giving birth so that their citizen children will be eligible for a full range of benefits available to every U.S. citizen. These mothers will someday petition on their behalf for their children to become permanent legal U.S. residents.

Birthright citizenship is an outgrowth of English common law that was ultimately adopted by the newly formed United States. The Fourteenth Amendment to our Constitution states as follows: "All persons born or naturalized in the United States, and subject to the jurisdiction thereof, are citizens of the United States and of the State wherein they reside." The big problem we have from the legal interpretation of this language is whether the authors of this Fourteenth Amendment intended to grant citizenship to the children of persons who have entered the country illegally, violated U.S. laws in the process, and have no allegiance or legitimate connection whatsoever to the United States.

Did you know that except for the United States, nearly every industrialized country in the world requires at least one parent to be a citizen or legal immigrant before a child born there becomes a citizen? Not a single European country automatically grants citizenship to the children of illegal immigrant parents. Many other countries have repealed the U.S.-style practices. This information was read into the congressional record by Representative Lamar Smith of Texas during a hearing of the Subcommittee on Immigration, Border Security and Claims. Representative Smith went on to make his point as to why birthright citizenship is such a concern by stating into the record that in 2004, "over one-half of all births in Los Angeles, our second-largest city, were to illegal immigrants." He further stated that, "once an illegal immigrant gives birth in the U.S., it is unlikely they will ever be deported and they can then sign up for federal, state, and local benefit programs, courtesy of the American taxpayer. This granting of automatic citizenship flows from a misinterpretation of the Fourteenth Amendment, as the Chairman pointed out in his opening statement. It was drafted after the Civil War to guarantee that the recently freed slaves rightfully received full citizenship rights. When it was enacted in 1868, there were no illegal immigrants in the United

States because there were no immigration laws until 1875, so drafters of the amendment could not have intended to benefit those in our country illegally." Every American taxpayer should be completely outraged by even the hint of the possibility of granting amnesty or citizenship to illegal immigrants or other non-U.S. citizens automatically.

The following estimated statistics have been compiled by ImmigrationCounters.com at *www.immigration.com* using the latest data from government and private sources, research, and other trending data:

- Current estimate of illegal immigrants in the United States: **21.9 million**

- Money wired to Mexico since January 2006: **$21.5 billion**

- Money wired to Latin America since 2001: **$214.3 billion**

- Cost of social services for illegal immigrants since 1996: **$397.4 billion**

- Children of illegal immigrants in our public schools: **4.6 million**

- Cost of illegals in school grades K-12 since 1996: **$13.7 billion**

- Illegal immigrants incarcerated in the United States: **389,000**

- Cost of Illegal immigrant incarceration since 2001: **$1.4 Billion**

- Illegal immigrant fugitives: **699,000**

- Anchor babies born in the US since 2002: **1.9 Million**

The statistics above should astonish every American, even if we assume that the amounts listed above are only half-true, as the annual cost to U.S. taxpayers is staggering.

Admittedly, there is no easy solution to this problem of illegal immigration, but it must be addressed immediately. U.S. taxpayers need to have a voice in any proposed resolutions, fully understanding the human side of any remedy on the entire population of illegal immigrants already here. They are not detected or registered anywhere for multiple years, with children born here and in U.S. schools, becoming mainstreamed. Perhaps some type of national vote (by verified U.S. citizens only) on the final proposed resolutions (see my recommendations below) may be the best path to take. Our elected representatives in Congress are afraid to take assertive action on this issue of great importance to all Americans because of possible fatal political fallout and public demonstrations. These are mostly organized and sponsored by the illegal immigrants themselves demanding rights. Please don't be shocked by this, as it has happened already many times in the United States, with the Mexican flag flying above the crowds in California, without an American flag in sight.

Did you know that for many years and through the completion of this book, many agencies in the major cities in the larger big-spend states have refused to exchange information with federal immigration officials or other law enforcement agencies about the activities or whereabouts of illegal immigrants? This fact is shocking indeed and has only changed slightly since 9/11, when it was revealed that the FBI, CIA, and police departments around the country never exchanged information that turned out to be vital to our individual safety and national security.

Some recommended measures that can be taken immediately include:

- Immediate deportation of any illegal immigrant guilty of committing a crime the nature of which would incarcerate a U.S. citizen who committed the same crime (excluding the crime of violating U.S. immigration laws, of course). Deportation would take effect upon release from prison.

- Have all illegal immigrants register with state and local authorities within a defined sixty-day period and thereafter be provided with identification cards that would include fingerprints, photo ID, and social security number so that a national database can be compiled in order for our government (and the taxpayers) to understand the true magnitude of the problem in terms of actual people involved, adults and children.

- Deny any type of social services or schooling to any illegal immigrant who fails to produce a valid U.S.-issued ID and is not registered with the state or local authorities, except in extreme medical emergencies, until formal registration is complete and verified in the proposed national database. Failure to register within six months of a date would be grounds for deportation.

- Impose heavy fines and revoke licenses of any employer that hires illegal immigrants who are not validly registered and able to produce the newly required government-issued alien identification card.

- Federal, state, and local governments, including all agencies and schools at every level, must cooperate and share any and all information available on illegal immigrants residing in their area, no exceptions.

- Automatic citizenship through amnesty will not be an option for any illegal residing in the United States due to the failure of government agencies not enforcing past or existing immigration laws.

- Elimination of birthright citizenship, especially when neither parent is a legal U.S. citizen. This was done in the UK and is being considered by many other countries.

- Complete building the wall along the borders with Mexico that was approved by Congress, and place federal or state National Guard troops at the country's land borders in the south. This is done in many other countries around the world, so why not here to stop the continuing invasion of illegal immigrants who may enter our country with a sickness or disease (such as tuberculosis) that may have already been eradicated in the U.S., **not to mention those who may slip in with ideas of committing acts of terror or other crimes?**

In fact, there are some additional matters to think about in terms of our Latin neighbors to the south that were presented in the 2008 Joint Operating Environment report prepared by the United States Joint Forces Command and found at *www. jfcom.mil/* and approved for public release on November 25, 2008. The report states that Mexico is on the verge of becoming unstable as its "government, its politicians, police and judicial infrastructure are all under sustained assault and pressure by criminal gangs and drug cartels." These same gangs and cartels "corrupt, distort, and damage the region's potential." An unstable Mexico could represent a serious "homeland security problem of immense proportions to the United States." **I must ask how it is possible that this very vital information has not been on the front pages of our domestic newspapers every day since its approval for public release?**

CONCLUSION:

We certainly need our political representatives in Washington to protect our southern borders, to safeguard the security of the United States. This is the primary responsibility of the federal government, and our politicians have been asleep at the wheel on this matter of national security for years. Think 9/11 right now!

The above recommendations can be a starting point in getting our arms around illegal immigration, its net cost to taxpayers, potential national security implications, and how to deal with it in a fair and equitable manner to all. I have intentionally avoided getting into many of the illegal immigration-specific arguments we read about in some newspapers, and would like to simply make everyone aware that there is a very substantial net tax cost to U.S. citizens. This taxpayer cost is in addition to all the changes that we have seen take place in many of our basic institutions adopting Spanish bilingual platforms. The changes include public schools, banking, telephone recordings, bilingual billings, Spanish voting materials and motor vehicle literature, to name a few without even thinking about the cost for all dual-language programs in both the private and public sectors.

One fact is undeniably true: United States citizens have not escaped the negative internal changes that have taken place here in our country that result from relaxed border controls and national security in exchange for cheaper unskilled labor.

Admittedly, most illegal immigrants are hard-working people who, for the most part, would stay in their own country if there were enough jobs that would allow them to earn a decent living and feed their families.

Our rewards as a nation for permitting this illegal immigration to continue unchecked are:

a. All aspects of our domestic business practices, including labor resources, education, and our culture in general are consistently being revised to incorporate Latino rather than maintaining an American standard.

b. We pay billions in extra tax dollars each year to fund a variety of social costs that come with this problem.

c. English as a second language is not far behind in the way of additional change that we should expect for many of our major cities throughout the country. In

New York, California and a growing number of states, Americans are finding it difficult to communicate with the help many vendors employ who simply can't speak or understand English. As a result, automated telephone assistance, ATM's and other forms of communication (including voting ballots) are offered in both English and Spanish,

d. The prospect of amnesty for the lawbreaking illegals would place more than 20 million people on the practically defunct social security system in the years to come.

e. Young Americans postpone having children that they currently cannot afford to both have and raise in the American tradition, while our taxes provide every imaginable service and subsidy to the children of illegal immigrants, at birth and forever after.

CHAPTER 6

WHERE THINGS STAND AND SOME RECOMMENDATIONS ON HOW WE MOVE FORWARD

As alluded to in the previous chapter, we began the year 2009 with a new U.S. president recently inaugurated, and our nation in very serious economic trouble.

The current financial crisis that our political representatives are trying to stabilize was born out of cumulative abuse, greed, failure to maintain effective regulatory oversight, extremely poor judgment on the part of government (federal, state, and local), financial executives in the banking/investment community, and many individuals.

In the ripple effect, international financial markets have also deteriorated significantly with the collapse, nationalization, or consolidation by many long-established financial and banking institutions that initially caused wholesale funding markets to almost completely shut down except for some very essential overnight access to funds. In a nutshell, the global banking community had a major seizure.

WHERE THINGS STAND AS OF EARLY FEBRUARY 2009

Let us take a look and summarize some of the key critical areas covered in chapters 1 through 5 impacting our daily lives. These things have collapsed right out from under us, causing severe financial harm to all citizens and the entire economic well-being of the United States as a whole.

1) First and foremost, government oversight and many regulatory agencies failed to exercise their primary responsibility to protect the citizens of the United States. When I use this term, *protect*, one must think of "national security" as multi-dimensional. Yes, our physical protection from hostile forces or terrorists violating our country's borders and citizens in some way is one dimension (perhaps the first and most important) for sure. A second dimension involves our internal economic well-being as a nation, with appropriate laws and regulations in place to prevent certain catastrophic events from occurring. A third dimension may involve

protection of the citizenry from widespread disease. A fourth dimension would protect us from an invasion of illegal immigrants crossing our borders unchecked. This brings about unexpected and significant taxpayer costs at all levels of government, drilling right down to the cities, towns, and villages in the form of additional school taxes to pay for the children of illegal immigrants enrolled in our schools.

2) The entire financial system, including the banking and investment industries, has gone into a tailspin. If it were not for the recent emergency intervention by the federal government, they would have completely collapsed for sure. In years past, and as recently as ten years ago, banks were much more regulated than they have been since 1999. Regulations and other controls were in place under the Glass Steagall Act of 1933 that for many years precluded banks from speculative and high-risk investing, in addition to setting up a regulatory firewall between commercial and investment bank activities.

Banks in general were the financial foundation of our society and viewed by many as the role model of how a business should be run with unquestioned integrity at every level. In those days past, the banks also had very strict standards and requirements before someone could qualify for a home or business loan. There were financial formulas that determined whether someone got the mortgage or not; no exceptions. Every prospective home buyer was required to come up with a down payment that was sufficient to ensure that their annual income would comfortably cover the monthly mortgage payments, including property taxes and insurance, in addition to preserving their ability to afford the basic essentials required such as food, utilities, commuting expenses, and the like. People trying to start up a business had to invest some of their own savings as equity to protect the bank in the event the business failed. These past requirements have either been significantly relaxed or abandoned altogether over the last ten to fifteen years, leaving both the U.S. banking and investment communities on life support.

3) The housing industry has been devastated by mortgage scandals and the abandonment of practices that made it a significant contributor to the economic success of the nation for many years since World War II. These practices deal with basic and reasonable mortgage qualification requirements (as described above), that were modified at the instigation and insistence of our very own elected congressional representatives in Washington.

Yes, expanded homeownership was good politics that many new homeowners would be happy about in the short term while interest rates were at historic lows and mortgage loan qualification only required that an applicant be breathing. No one considered the risks that unaffordable homeownership would bring about, not only to the new homeowner but to the nation in the form of a near total collapse of our entire financial system. How can anyone condone the mortgage product that existed through the middle of 2007 known as the "NINJA" requiring no income, no job, and no assets for the applicant to qualify for a mortgage? Many recent homeowners, especially the NINJA applicants, are now seeing their dream home lost to foreclosure proceedings. Finally, let's not forget the poor U.S. legal citizen taxpayers, their children and grandchildren, who get stuck with the bill for all these risky mortgage blunders that now translate into substantial national bailout debt in the trillions of dollars.

4) The U.S. auto industry, including GM, Ford, and Chrysler, is on the verge of bankruptcy due to onerous union contractual wage and benefits obligations that have made them unable to compete with lower-cost foreign auto manufacturers for decades.

5) Consumer credit, a key driver in our economy, has dried up due to the banking crisis. Most lending is at a virtual standstill, impacting business borrowings, mortgages, car loans, home equity lines, credit cards, and all other areas of credit so essential to our economic machine.

6) In the year 2008, more than 2.6 million people have lost their jobs, and there were 11 million people out of work at the end of that year, allowing the unemployment rate to reach 7.2 percent. The year-end government labor report also stated that the 2008 drop in employment was the highest since 1945, with more significant job losses expected in the month of January 2009 and beyond.

7) Federal, state, and local tax collections are down billions of dollars, while most of the cost to keep the various levels of government running is fixed with items such as payroll and benefits. On top of this fixed cost, we are saddled with many costly programs in place, including Medicaid, Medicare, food stamps, aid to schools, welfare, daycare, and the cost of illegal immigration, to name a few. Many states have already forecast budget deficits in the billions of dollars over the next several years; everyone is looking to Uncle Sam for a bailout rather than dealing with the very necessary severe spending cuts. This will no doubt require either public-sector pay cuts or layoffs, in

addition to across-the-board cuts covering a wide range of state and local services provided.

8) Unemployment funds in many states are depleted.

9) Pension funds in many of the larger states and cities have lost billions of dollars in value due to the 2008 stock market crash. These losses will regrettably require additional taxpayer funding for many years to come, on top of all the other existing tax burdens.

10) Personal spending is down as many people are in shock, having experienced most of their life savings evaporate due to the market crash and a substantial decline in the value of their home.

11) The country is going deep into debt in an effort to stabilize the financial banking system. Many industries tied into the aftermath of the banking collapse have announced personnel layoffs as business activities decline dramatically due to credit availability drying up.

12) There is widespread concern that the federal government has not yet come up with the required solution to the economic crisis despite the commitment of almost 2 trillion dollars representing new national debt that will need to be paid back by taxpayers sometime in the future. This concern has translated into rapidly declining confidence in our elected Washington leadership.

13) A second more compelling related fear is that the recent stimulus bill passed by Congress and signed into law by the new president in late February 2009 will not help the economy genuinely recover. The bill includes mostly state bailout funds and welfare-type non-productive program payments and other expenditures that save more existing jobs rather than creating new ones. This would render the program ineffective, compounding the current problems and costing much more in the years to come, just to correct the bad spending decisions included in the stimulus package.

14) We are now, and have been for many years, a nation totally dependent on foreign sources for our complete energy needs. Our political representatives have campaigned on platforms of reducing this energy dependence since the early 1970s, but to date very little has been done. Each month, hundreds of millions of U.S. dollars are sent to foreign producers of the crude oil we consume.

15) Illegal immigrants here in the United States numbering more than 20 million are a very severe drain on federal, state, and local budgets through services provided including health care, schools, welfare, food stamps and a host of other programs, all at U.S. citizen taxpayer

expense. The cost is no doubt staggering and almost impossible to quantify with any degree of accuracy because we just don't know how many such illegal immigrants are actually here. A census would be very helpful in this regard.

16) Since December 2008, the Hospital Workers and Teachers Unions in New York are spending millions of dollars on TV ads (funded by dues of the working members, of course). These ads proclaim that the governor should not cut aid to schools or hospitals that will cause job layoffs and have a terrible effect on care and services that will in some way impact the welfare of our children. These ads are naturally scare tactics and totally insensitive to what is currently going on in the private sector of our economy. Millions of workers have not only lost their jobs but lost substantial 401(k) pension savings in the market decline as well.

I would like to make the point here that it has become very common for union leaders and politicians to mention frequently that the children are being victimized whenever spending cuts are mentioned. They claim the cuts will imperil their educational needs and future well-being. The quality of the educational system in this country has been deteriorating for many years, despite the spending of billions and billions in extra tax dollars on so many different programs. No one is being held accountable for this continuous erosion in the quality of education. Many children graduating from high school and even college are very deficient in both oral and written communication skills, to the dismay of prospective employers. Most of these same students are also deficient in subjects such as geography, American history, sociology, economics, and politics, all subjects very essential for making many decisions in life. The public schools have failed because they have become a bureaucratic nightmare and socialist in their approach to education.

In my opinion, one of the biggest contributing factors to this overall education problem in our country is that students are not getting the much-needed parental support and encouragement at home for academic achievement. Parents expect teachers to perform miracles in the classroom with their children. Proper education of our young is a continuous effort, starting at a very early age in the home and thereafter reinforced at both school and home for many years. Parents must ensure that children complete their homework assignments, and must help them with difficult subjects if necessary, to emphasize the importance of education. This apparent severe lack of parental involvement and assistance at home—especially for students at inner-city schools—totally undermines the teacher's efforts. This condition also diminishes the child's overall view and attitude toward education in general. Consequently, educators have an uphill battle, with students severely lacking basic disciplines that include respect for educators (and other adults as well). Teachers should not object to reinforcing basic individual values (that should be first taught in the home by parents who decided to have children in the first place) such as responsibility, accountability, honesty, self-control, respect for elders, and obeying the rules and laws of society in general, to name a few. Many of our young suffer from an entitlement expectation disorder of unknown origin. Please see item 19 later on in chapter 6, where you will read about the many billions of additional dollars (representing new taxpayer debt) that will be provided to various education programs in the states by the proposed new economic stimulus bill. The grants in their present form contain no specific goals to improve the overall quality of education in this country that has been declining for many years. This has occurred despite huge increases in education expenditures year after year paid for by the poor legal citizen taxpayers in this country.

17) The *New York Post* newspaper reported in its Sunday, February 8, 2009 edition that "more than 70 percent of the retiring firefighters in the past five years did so on disabilities hiking the cost of taxpayer-funded FDNY pensions to nearly $1 billion a year." A normal pension is one-half pay after twenty years, using the last three years of base pay plus overtime earnings. This normal pension is exempt from state and city income taxes, but not federal income taxes. The disability pension, on the other hand, is based on 75 percent of the firefighter base pay plus overtime and is exempt from federal as well as state and city income taxes. Many firefighters and other uniformed civil servants in many large cities arrange to work substantial overtime in the last three years of their career, with the sole purpose of inflating their pension benefit. State legislators have looked the other way and permitted this abuse for many years in return for political support from the unions and their members directly benefiting from the practice. I am the first to admit that the firefighters and other first responders are brave and do a terrific job, routinely facing danger. However, they do receive an excellent salary and benefits, including

generous pensions and medical care benefits to begin with. So why is the overtime abuse so embedded in the system? Perhaps our elected officials are not monitoring this substantial taxpayer cost properly. In many instances, the voter taxpayers are never told in advance what union negotiations will cost once the contracts with the unions have been agreed to and therefore cannot object timely. Please refer back to chapter 3 dealing with state spending out of control, wherein I reported how a Westchester County correction officer had so much overtime that he likely set the stage to receive a pension of at least $113,626 per year for 20 years of service and possibly $170,439 per year if he had 30 years of service. All taxpayer-funded, of course, and assuming he does not go out on disability, enriching the retirement benefit even more.

18) We are involved in what appears to be an endless, expanding war in the Middle East involving Iraq, Afghanistan, and Pakistan, with other neighboring countries on the verge of being dragged in to the fray.

19) In early 2009, our new Democratic president, with a Democratic-controlled Congress, concluded that a new (second) and more urgent federal economic stimulus plan was vital, following the near collapse of the U.S.

banking system. The communicated thrust of the new stimulus plan is to create more jobs, provide money to the many states facing massive budget deficits, and stimulate economic activities in both the private and public sectors. The problem many U.S. taxpaying citizens have with the proposed House and Senate plans is that most of the $800 billion plus in spending has very little direct relationship to genuine economic expansion. *All readers must keep foremost in their mind that all federal government spending programs require the country to take on additional debt that ultimately must be paid back in the future over many years by the taxpayers, including the interest on the debt.*

Below is a listing of selective proposed spending items contained in the House proposed version of the new stimulus bill that has very little to do with creation of new jobs and stimulating the economy.

- Food stamps—**$20 billion.**
- Public housing assistance—**$7.5 billion.**
- Nutrition programs—**$1 billion.**
- ACORN—**$6 billion**—ACORN represents a collection of political action groups that were involved with multiple voting irregularities during the most recent presidential

election and a major advocate of the mortgage housing programs that in part contributed to the banking crisis in this country.

- **$1 billion** for Amtrak, the national rail service provider.

- **$400 million** for global warming-related projects.

- **$50 million** in grants to the National Endowment for the Arts.

- **$22.9 billion** for Rural Housing Insurance Fund Program.

- **$100 Million** for Food and Nutrition Service for Women, Infants, and Children; does not state if this program is for U.S. citizens only, nor does it exclude illegal immigrants and their illegally born children here in the United States.

- **$3 billion** for state and local law enforcement with no specific requirement for new jobs.

- **$1 billion** for Community Oriented Policing Services, covering hiring and rehiring of additional career law-enforcement officers.

- **$2.5 billion** for academic research facilities modernization.

- **$8 billion** for Innovative Technology Loan Guarantee Program, with $25 million solely earmarked to administer the program.

- **$8.4 billion** for State and Tribal Assistance Grants for clean-water capitalization projects, including $2 billion for safe water drinking programs.

- **$4 billion** for training and employment services—no mention of new jobs, only that $1.2 billion is for states to fund youth activities including summer jobs, and $1 billion for dislocated worker employment and training activities, $750 million for a program of competitive grants for "worker training and placement in high growth and emerging industry sectors."

- **$2.2 billion** for Department of Health and Human Services, with $500 million in grants to public health centers, with no restrictions such as "services for legal U.S. citizens only"; and $600 million for training of nurses and primary-care physicians and dentists.

- **$1 billion** for low-income home energy assistance that includes assistance with heating bills. There is no language in this area of the stimulus bill that limits this bucket of benefits to only legal citizens of the United States, nor does it exclude illegal non-U.S. citizens from receiving such assistance.

- **$2 billion** in payments to states for the Child Care and Development Block Grant. No new jobs come out of this appropriation, and no language in the area of the stimulus bill limits this bucket of benefits to only legal citizens of the United States, nor does it exclude illegal non-U.S. citizens from receiving such services

- **$3.2 billion** for children and family services programs, including a) $2.1 billion for the Head Start programs. Head Start is a national program that promotes school readiness by enhancing the social and cognitive development of children through the provision of educational, health, nutritional, social, and other services to enrolled children and families. No new jobs come out of this appropriation, and there is no language in this area of the stimulus bill that limits this bucket of benefits to only legal citizens of the United States, nor does it exclude illegal non-U.S. citizens from receiving such services; and b) $1 billion for unspecified community services and other community activities. Not a single mention of job creation.

- **$13 billion** for the education of the disadvantaged, with only $2 billion of this amount for school improvements. Where is the remaining $11 billion being spent, I ask, and who specifically are the disadvantaged? Please let's have a list of the groups and whether it includes children of illegal immigrant non-citizens, as there is presently no language in this area of the stimulus bill limiting this bucket of benefits to only legal citizens of the United States, nor does it exclude illegal non-U.S. citizens from receiving such services. No new jobs are created from this appropriation.

- **$13.6 billion** for special education, with not a single hint of any job creation whatsoever. Again, there is presently no language in this area of the stimulus bill limiting this bucket of benefits to only legal citizens of the United States, nor does it exclude illegal non-U.S. citizens from receiving such services.

- **$16.1 billion** for "student financial assistance," with funds available through September 30, 2011. Not a dollar for any type of capital expenditures that would create some temporary jobs is included within this huge pool of funds, with no permanent jobs. Again, there is no language in this area of the stimulus bill limiting this pool of benefits to only legal citizens of the United States, nor does it exclude illegal non-U.S. citizens from receiving such services.

- **$14 billion** for school modernization, renovation, and repair, with $6 billion solely for administration and oversight of the program. How this is at all possible that almost half of this pool will go to administer the program is a red flag, with not a single permanent job created and no mention of the personnel who will be charged with this administrative responsibility.

- **$1 billion** for community planning and development, with no mention of potential new job creation or language in this area of the stimulus bill limiting this bucket of benefits to only legal citizens of the United States, nor does it exclude illegal non-U.S. citizens from receiving such services.

- **$4.2 billion** in additional community development funds to be used for neighborhood stabilization activities related to emergency assistance for the redevelopment of abandoned and foreclosed homes. No new permanent jobs can be expected from this appropriation, nor is there language in this area of the stimulus bill limiting this bucket of benefits to only legal citizens of the United States or exclusionary language for illegal non-U.S. citizens from receiving such services.

- **$1.5 Billion** for homeless assistance grants, including short- and long-term rental assistance, housing relocation, housing searches, medication, and outreach to property owners, legal services, credit repair, utility payments, moving costs, and other appropriate homelessness prevention activities. **No new jobs come from this expenditure for sure or language limiting such benefits to only U.S. citizens who have lost their jobs or homes. What this means to me is that funds will be available to illegal immigrants and their families, especially since the secretary of Housing and Urban Development may waive statutory or regulatory provisions related to the obligation and use of such funds. Wow! If that doesn't kill or fry Joe the Taxpayer's brain, nothing will.**

- **$79 billion** for state fiscal stabilization to be administered by the Department of Education. All this money is to keep the schools in the various states spending at current levels without new job creation required or any cuts in unnecessary spending programs. The bulk of this money will be used to avoid job cuts in the states and cities without a single new job created. It is also unlikely that the state taxpayers will escape tax increases in multiple areas such as school, property, sales, income, and other nuisance taxes that are necessary to curtail and limit in some way the massive mounting deficits in many of the larger states.

The above partial listing of proposed stimulus plan expenditures is what is in the forefront of my mind and should enrage all taxpayers. They make up the largest portion of the spending proposals that clearly represent nothing more than a massive welfare-type spending spree. Are we to believe that this is the best resolution to the financial crisis that our elected officials can come up with? The entire bill, including all the above items was passed by the Congress with virtually no changes to the bill I read in conducting the research for this book, including the excerpted items listed above.

SOME RECOMMENDATIONS ON HOW WE MIGHT MOVE FORWARD

In an attempt to make this closing section of the book a platform for all the newly informed taxpayers, I will be both specific and brief with my suggested remedies and remind everyone that it will certainly not be an all-inclusive list, but a good start for the Washington and other state and local legislative double talkers.

TAXATION

Immediately reduce the U.S. federal corporate income tax rate to 25 percent from 35 percent. This tax reduction will have the following results:

1) Large and small businesses will re-invest the new untaxed dollars and expand their business in a way that will genuinely create permanent jobs.

2) The business growth will expand the tax base and increase the funds flowing into the United States Treasury in the form of new taxes. States will also benefit from this expansion.

3) Lower domestic corporate tax rates will make U.S.-based companies more competitive in the global arena and also attract foreign investors that were otherwise investing in countries with lower tax rates and other investing incentives in place.

4) Make the Bush administration individual income tax rate cuts permanent. This will provide taxpayers with more disposable income that will drive economic growth.

5) Reduce the capital gains tax rate to 10 percent from the current 15 percent. The last cut in this tax generated hundreds of millions in new tax dollars, as investors were willing to take gains and pay reasonable taxes, with most of the proceeds moving on to new investments.

6) Reinstate the investment tax credit that will encourage business to immediately invest in new plants and equipment that will help with economic growth and expansion.

7) Provide a $5,000 jobs credit to all employers for each newly hired employee who keeps the new job for at least 24 months.

8) Request that employers reduce employee benefits costs or perhaps even cut salaries as an alternative to job eliminations that reduce the population of taxpayers.

9) Provide a $15,000 annual tax credit for all stay-at-home moms with a working spouse and children below primary school age. The cost for this benefit would be partially funded by savings from the child care credit and reduced day care expense subsidies that would not be used. This tax credit proposal is designed to encourage young mothers to stay home and raise their young children, to promote and rekindle family values that have long been abandoned. This program would also deliver children with far fewer emotional issues or handicaps into the school system and should substantially reduce the overall cost of education per child to the taxpayers.

<u>ENERGY</u>

Everyone must understand that while we as a nation attempt to develop multiple sources of alternative energy, we will still be heavily reliant on crude oil (fossil fuel) for at least the next twenty-five to fifty years. The politicians have been talking about energy independence since the early 1970s when we imported some 20 to 25 percent of our energy needs in the form of crude oil. We are now importing more than 60 percent of our energy needs in the form of crude oil while our potential reserves in coastal waters and the ANWR remain hands-off because of baseless "politically correct" environmental concerns. I and many fellow Americans who would love to have the country more energy independent also have sincere concerns about damage to the environment. I love my clean East Coast beaches and waters that provide us with joy, but there must be a limit to this development oil and gas drilling restraint that has caused this great nation of ours to become very dependent on foreign sources for our energy needs. We have the best and safest offshore and onshore drilling record in the entire world. There is more oil pollution caused by oil seeping naturally out of untapped reservoirs that need to be tapped when compared to the very few incidents involving oil spills that have taken place over the past fifty years. We as a nation have experienced virtually no pollution from actual offshore exploration or drilling activities. The oil spill in Alaskan waters many years ago was caused by an intoxicated oil tanker captain and not drilling or production activities. Also, please keep in mind that our Florida coastal waters are off limits to drilling, while China is set to drill in the waters in and about Cuba. Hopefully the Chinese and Cubans will be half as diligent in their approach to exploratory drilling and development as required by our own stringent federal regulations established for such activities with remarkable success to date in the prevention of offshore spills and pollution.

Congress should immediately lift all restrictions on drilling in our coastal waters and portions of the ANWR. This action will accomplish the following:

1) Create tens of thousands of jobs in multiple locations throughout the United States.

2) Reduce the substantial outflow of U.S. dollars each month to foreign crude oil producers that satisfy our energy requirements. The hundreds of billions of dollars will thus remain here in the States for reinvestment by the U.S.- based oil companies in alternative energy projects, simultaneously expanding our economy and tax base. The increased billions of dollars that will be collected by the federal and state governments from royalties, production taxes, and the like should be used to help pay off some of the trillions in debt we find ourselves in due to the recent financial crisis.

3) Encourage the private construction of new crude oil refineries in economically depressed areas of our country near the Canadian and Mexican borders. That will allow for imports from those countries to be processed in the areas closest to the point of entry into the United

States. Western New York State, Michigan, and other locations would be ideal and also help with the growing unemployment conditions in the named states. We have not built a new petroleum refinery in this country since the late 1970s and early 1980s. This new construction will help alleviate refined product availability and distribution problems and the annual supply bottlenecks we experience when refineries have to switch gears and refine crude into more heating oil and less gasoline. It will take years to build such refineries and create thousands of new jobs in the process.

4) Require the construction of new nuclear power plants in multiple areas of the United States, creating permanent jobs in the private sector and further expanding the income tax base.

5) Designate thousands of federal acres in the Great Plains as wind power zones, available for development by privately owned corporations or other domestic investors, and not funded by tax dollars from Joe the Taxpayer. This private capital investment encouraged by the federal government through leasing of federal lands and perhaps tax incentives will create thousands of permanent new jobs and new taxpayers.

6) Encourage the development of additional hydroelectric power plants with tax incentives for capital investment

in such facilities.

7) Encourage the additional development and production of shale oil and coal-extraction facilities, again with tax-driven investment incentives that have always proved successful in the past.

ILLEGAL IMMIGRATION

I cannot believe how the very serious problem of illegal immigration into the United States has not been a subject of more frequent ongoing discussions and debates over the past fifteen or twenty years by our politicians at every level of government. Moreover, the news media has not taken up this problem in making the taxpayers of this country aware of the profound effects such immigration has had on our communities, schools, business culture, and individual tax burdens.

All this "let's not touch on or deal with the subject of illegal immigration" needs to be changed immediately by demanding corrective actions as set forth below by our elected federal government representatives who each have a primary sworn duty to protect and defend the United States of America. *The United States of America is us—the legal citizens and taxpayers all.*

1) Demand that all services of every type, including schooling, medical (exception for life-threatening medical care only),

welfare, food stamps to illegal immigrants and their children, who may or may not be legal citizens, cease immediately until all such persons have been registered with local authorities, fingerprinted, and placed into a national database accessible by every federal, state, and local government agency including law enforcement, schools, motor vehicle bureaus and so on, This will allow us all to know who is walking our streets, attending our schools, increasing our taxes, and taking jobs from legal citizens, especially at this time with a major recession in full swing, an unemployment rate approaching double digits and more that 6 million jobs lost since the Summer of 2008.

2) I do not advocate the immediate deportation of the millions of illegal immigrants who are already here in the United States to work hard and not commit crimes on our streets. However, I do expect that they all be registered with federal agencies, provided with photo and fingerprint ID cards, and given a free taxpayer-funded medical check-up to ensure they are not bringing infectious, dangerous diseases into our country. A final requirement is to have them each apply for individual tax identification numbers (ITIN). The ITIN is a tax processing number only available for certain non-resident and resident aliens, their spouses, and dependents who cannot get a social security number (SSN) that would entitle them to benefits under the program. It is a nine-digit number, beginning

with the number 9, and formatted like an SSN (XXX-XX-XXXX). This ITIN will allow the aliens to work without the requirement of having a social security number or entitlement to social security or Medicare benefits down the road. This is a compromise price for breaking and entering into our country illegally. Details about the ITIN can be found at *www.irs.gov.*

3) Do not grant any illegal immigrant amnesty per se, but allow them to continue working as agricultural or other unskilled laborers here in the United States for a maximum period of ten months per year, followed by a mandatory return to their country of origin for at least two months per year. Thereafter, they can return for additional ten-month work periods without limit by simply producing their photo ID and ITIN.

4) Secure our borders to the south by placing federal troops at the borders of each border state that has served as an entry gateway for Latin and South American illegal immigrants.

5) Mandate through federal regulations that employers of documented unskilled alien workers (formerly illegal immigrants) can only hire such individuals for not longer than a consecutive ten months, paying them at an hourly rate of not less than the minimum wage plus a predetermined untaxed fixed amount contributed into a medical care fund for the exclusive benefit of alien workers. The employer must also withhold all legally required income and payroll taxes. All such

persons can be rehired by the same employer upon their return to the United States from the mandatory two-month vacation in their country of origin.

6) Children born to female documented foreign unskilled workers will not be granted citizenship as a matter of law.

7) Encourage the use of the English language at all times by limiting Spanish accommodation literature at all government agencies, schools, and places of employment.

The above measures will substantially reduce the taxpayer cost related to the more than 20 million illegal immigrants currently in the United States, draining services in many states and cities throughout the country. Additionally, and as stated previously, many of our own young couples here in the United States (all citizens and many likely the children and grandchildren of combat veterans who fought to preserve our basic American liberties) cannot afford to have children and therefore postpone having families, while the income taxes they pay fund all types of benefits and other services for the babies born to illegal immigrants. Something is very wrong with this picture.

FEDERAL, STATE, AND LOCAL GOVERNMENTS

1) Demand that all annual budgets be limited to the

most recent fiscal year tax collections and any other government revenue sources such as royalties, bonus payments for leases, sale of government property, and the like.

2) Demand that all state and local public payroll expenses, including benefits and pensions, be limited to comparable salaries and benefits programs in the private sector.

3) Demand that actions be taken to eliminate all public pension abuses, including severe limits on overtime, in arriving at entitled retirement benefits that have contributed to substantial increases in taxes for all taxpayers.

4) In order to reduce deficits at the state and local levels of government brought about by declining revenues, rather than increase taxes from already overburdened taxpayers, seek ways to cut costs either through job reductions, or in the alternative cut salaries by 5, 10, 15 percent or more if needed. In addition, renegotiation of benefits commitments that will bring overall costs down to a level supported by incoming tax revenues without increasing taxes should be a standard rule at all times.

The above four groupings dealing with suggested changes in the areas of taxation, energy policy, illegal immigration, and the manner in which federal, state, and local officials spend taxpayer money would quickly put us on the fast track to economic recovery. The big question is whether politicians will rise to the occasion and for once be true "statesmen" and put the best interests of our country first, not cater to special interest groups, and especially not worry about what the mainstream media may not think is "politically correct."

We must therefore insist on immediate changes in the way our government presently conducts the affairs of our great nation.

ABOUT THE AUTHOR

He is a financial professional very concerned about how federal, state and local taxes are rising unnoticed by most American citizens with more increases on the way following the 2008 financial crisis and the enormous government spending that followed to hopefully bring about stability to the banking and financial industries. Many taxpayers don't even know how many different forms of tax are emptying their pockets every day from so many sources. As a licensed CPA with an MBA in taxation, he is attempting to provide the reader with a better understanding of where all this tax money is going and how we might be able to stop the increases year after year.